Better Homes and Gardens®

plumbing
Step-by-Step

Meredith® Books
Des Moines, Iowa

TABLE OF CONTENTS

Planning FOR PLUMBING   12

Minor Improvements AND REPAIRS   18

Major Improvements
AND REPAIRS 84

Tools
AND MATERIALS 128

Plumbing
SKILLS 140

If you own a home, you'll eventually face some sort of plumbing job, whether it be a dripping faucet or a complete bathroom makeover. Most people assume plumbing is dirty and difficult and requires skills gained only by years of experience. Fear of the unknown drives them to pay hundreds and even thousands of dollars to plumbers to do jobs they might easily handle themselves. Even when homeowners hire out jobs legitimately beyond their skill level, they're often left wondering whether the job was done right—and for a fair price.

Step-by-Step Plumbing explains how your plumbing system works and what it takes to tackle most household repairs and improvements. In simple, step-by-step fashion it explains how to fix minor and major problems and how to install new plumbing fixtures in a professional manner.

Perhaps best of all, *Step-by-Step Plumbing* will help you evaluate what you can take on yourself. You'll find that plumbing can be a budget-sparing and satisfying way to improve your home. If you choose to call in the pros, you'll be equipped to manage the job wisely.

How to use this book
Get inspired! Pages 12–17 show the creative side of plumbing. Browse through these pages to see what others have done and to develop your own remodeling ideas.

Stay safe. Begin by reading "Safety" and "Permits and Codes" on pages 6–7. Become familiar with overall safety procedures to ensure you work safely from the very beginning of every project. You'll also find "Caution" boxes throughout the book that help you remain safe as you complete a particular project. In addition, "Permits and Codes" provides information describing when you'll be required to obtain a building permit or meet codes on a plumbing project. It's critical that you check with your local building department before beginning a project so that your plans can be approved, and so you'll know at what stages the project will need to be inspected. "Getting to Know Your System" on pages 8–11 provides general knowledge to help you understand the parts of your home's structure. Learn about the three fundamental plumbing systems in your home: the supply system, the drain system, and the vent system.

The next two chapters, "Minor Improvements and Repairs" and "Major Improvements," discuss specific projects. You need not read all of these pages until you plan to undertake one of those projects. These chapters will introduce you to a variety of popular repairs and upgrades, from fixing a toilet that won't stop running to installing a tub and whirlpool. Look through these chapters for ideas to enhance your home. Each project contains a "You'll Need" box that details approximately how long a project will take, what skills are required to complete it, and

what tools are necessary.

The "Tools and Materials" chapter offers information that will help you choose the tools you need or want and acquaints you with the materials and hardware available to you.

If you want to learn new plumbing skills or brush up on current ones, read the final chapter, "Plumbing Skills," to get an idea of the basic procedures involved in most plumbing projects. This chapter shows the proper use and care of plumbing tools and the proper techniques for using them safely and effectively. It's always a good idea to practice seldom-used skills and techniques before beginning an actual project.

Tip boxes

In addition to the basic instructions and the "You'll Need" information boxes, you'll find plenty of additional tips throughout the book. Pay special attention to the "Caution" boxes—they warn when a how-to step requires special care. They will help keep you from doing damage to yourself or to your home.

Other information boxes provide helpful hints—tricks of the trade from experts, tips on how to cut costs, and ideas to organize a job to minimize wasted time, labor, and materials. They all help you complete your plumbing project quickly, safely, and easily, to turn your home improvement dreams into reality.

STYLE AND FUNCTION
Installing a new vanity, sink, and faucet can be the first steps in remodeling an outdated bathroom. The projects in this book will walk you through each step necessary to achieve the end results you desire.

Working safely

You can do any plumbing project, but use common sense and follow the instructions when using any solvents or working with drainpipes. Drainpipes transport wastewater from the home. Wastewater contains biohazards and generates hazardous gases. Take the proper precautions when working with a live system.

Goggles or safety glasses are an absolute must. They protect your eyes from debris when cutting, pounding, soldering, or working above your head. Just as important, they protect you from splashing liquids when working with plumbing drainage systems and fixtures.

Wear a respirator when working in a poorly ventilated area. Gases produced from waste or working with hazardous chemicals can be dangerous when inhaled. Make sure you use the correct respirator. Check the manufacturer's specifications.

Proper ventilation is important when working with or around gases such as natural gas or carbon monoxide. An odorant is added to natural gas by the local utility so that you can identify if you have a leak. If you suspect a natural gas leak, open as many windows as possible. Don't operate any electrical switches. Call your local utility for assistance. Carbon monoxide (CO) is an odorless, colorless, and tasteless gas; it therefore presents a grave danger. Any appliance that uses a fuel-burning source can produce carbon monoxide. CO detectors are available and can be a valuable addition to your home. You may even receive a discount on your home insurance rates for installing one.

Protect your skin

Caustic solutions can burn the skin. Wastewater contains biohazards that can enter the skin. Wear long-sleeve shirts and pants. Launder clothing immediately after use.

Gloves protect the hands. Wear them to protect against cuts as well as contact with chemicals. When working with chemicals, read the label to be sure the gloves you have will provide the necessary protection.

Tool safety tips

Safety is the result of following guidelines and exercising common sense. When working with a powerful electric tool, just one moment's lapse of concentration can lead to disaster. To minimize risks with power tools, keep the following guidelines in mind:

■ Use tools only for the jobs they were designed to do. If a tool came with an instruction manual, take the time to read it to find out what the tool will do and what it will not do.

■ Check on the condition of a tool before using it. A dull cutting edge or loose-fitting hammer head, for example, spells trouble. Also inspect the cord of a power tool to make sure it's not damaged.

■ Don't work with tools if you're tired or in a hurry.

■ Don't work with tools if you have been recently drinking alcoholic beverages.

■ Wear goggles whenever the operation you are performing could result in an eye injury.

■ The safety mechanisms on power tools are there for your protection. Do not tamper with or remove them from the tool.

■ Do not wear loose-fitting clothes or dangling jewelry while you are using tools.

■ Keep people, especially children, at a safe distance while you're using any tool. Before you allow a child to use a tool, instruct them on how to operate it. Never allow a child to use a tool without proper adult supervision.

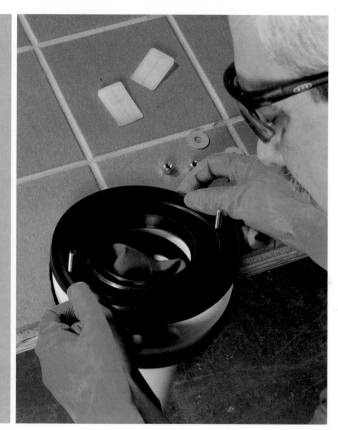

TAKE SAFETY PRECAUTIONS Plumbing systems not only bring clean water to your home, but transport wastes from your home. Wastewater generates hazardous gases. Take the necessary safety precautions, such as wearing gloves, ventilating work areas, and practicing general safe work habits.

PERMITS AND CODES

Working to code

You may be an amateur working on your own house, but you have the same responsibilities as a licensed plumber. The plumbing elements you repair or install must provide a supply of pure and wholesome water and must facilitate the safe passage of liquids, solid wastes, and gases out of your house. This means that you must use only those techniques and materials that are acceptable under the building codes in your area.

The procedures in this book represent the editors' understanding of the Uniform Plumbing Code (UPC). Local codes are based on this uniform code but can vary greatly from each other. If no local codes cover the work you will be doing, consult the national codes. You'll find the latest edition of the UPC in the reference section of the library. If local codes do cover your project, they supersede any national requirements. (Canadian residents can obtain a copy of the Canadian Plumbing Code by contacting Publications Sales M-20, National Research Council of Canada, Ottawa, K1A 0R6 Ontario.)

Working with your local building department

Consult with your local building department if you plan to add or change your plumbing in any substantial way or if you believe the existing plumbing might be substandard. Plumbing codes may seem bothersome, but they are designed to make your home's plumbing system safe and worry-free. Those who ignore codes often make costly mistakes, create health hazards, and can have difficulty selling their homes later on.

If you will be adding new service—not just replacing one fixture with another one—check with your building department before proceeding. Neglecting to do so could cost you the expense and trouble of tearing out and redoing your work.

The inspector who comes to your house may be helpful, friendly, and flexible, or a real stickler. But no matter what, your job will proceed more smoothly if you follow these guidelines:

- To avoid asking unnecessary questions, find out as much pertinent information as possible about your project before you talk to an inspector. Your building department may offer literature concerning your type of installation. If not, consult national codes.

- Go to your inspector with a plan to be approved or amended; don't expect the building department to plan the job for you.

- Present your plan with neatly drawn diagrams and a complete list of the materials you will use.

- Be sure you clearly understand when you need to have inspections. Do not cover up any work that needs to be inspected.

- Be as courteous as possible. Inspectors are often wary of homeowners, because so many are ignorant of codes and procedures. Show the inspector you are serious about doing things the right way and comply with any requirements without argument.

CHECK CODES
Installing a tub or whirlpool is not a task you want to immediately redo to fix a code violation. Check local building codes before you begin a plumbing project to ensure you proceed according to code the first time.

GETTING TO KNOW YOUR SYSTEM

With so many pipes and fittings behind walls and under floors, a plumbing system seems complicated and mysterious to the inexperienced. But plumbing is actually a straightforward matter of distributing clean, incoming water to where it's wanted and facilitating the outflow of waste. Here's an overview of how household plumbing works.

Supply, drain, and vent systems

The supply system brings water into your house, divides it into hot and cold water lines, and distributes it to various fixtures (sinks, toilets, showers, tubs) and appliances (washing machines, dishwashers, water heaters, heating system boilers).

The drain system carries water away from the fixtures and appliances, and out of the house.

The vent system supplies air to the drainpipes so waste flows out freely. Because drains and vents use the same types of pipes and are tied together, they often are referred to as the drain-waste-vent system or DWV.

Locating the water meter and main shutoffs

The first step toward mastering your house's plumbing system is to locate the water meter and the main shutoff.

Look for the place where the water supply enters your house. In most cases a pipe an inch or so thick, called a water main, comes up through the floor in the basement or on the first floor. If you have metered water, the pipe enters and exits a round gauge, the water meter, which has either a digital readout that looks like a car's odometer or a series of five or six dials. The meter records how much water passes into the house. If you have a well, or if your bill stays the same no matter how much water you use, you don't have a meter.

Near the place where the water main enters your house, you'll find one or two valves that you can turn on and off by hand. This is the main shutoff for the house.

An additional shutoff may be located outside the house buried in a compartment sometimes called a buffalo box. To find it, look for a round metal cover in the ground near the street or the edge of your property. (It may be overgrown with grass.) Pry up the cover and look inside with a flashlight. There you'll find a valve that you can turn by hand or one that requires a special long-handled key. Older homes in warm-weather localities sometimes have an exposed valve just outside the house.

If you have an older home, don't depend entirely on the inside shutoff; it can break, leak, or fail completely. If you need to shut down the system often during a project, learn where the outside shutoff is and use it to shut off the water.

CAUTION

KNOW HOW TO SHUT OFF THE WATER

In case of a burst pipe or other emergency, be ready to shut off the main water supply quickly. Show members of your family where the main shutoff is. Clear away boxes and furniture so it is easy to reach. If it takes a special tool to shut off your water, keep that tool handy.

WHERE YOUR RESPONSIBILITY ENDS

The water meter is the continental divide for assigning responsibility for plumbing repairs. The water meter and pipes leading away from the house are the responsibility of the water company, and the water company should fix them for free. Anything on the house side of the meter is the homeowner's responsibility. However, if you plan to add new fixtures (not just replacing old ones), your municipality might require that a larger water main come into the house. If so, you'll have to pay for it. Check when you get your permit.

THE NEW AND THE OLD

In the old days, plumbers installed cast-iron drain lines. They packed each joint with tarred oakum, then poured in molten lead—a practice that dates back to the Ancient Romans. For supply lines and smaller drain lines, they used galvanized pipe, which is strong but rusts and corrodes over time.

Plastic drain lines and copper supply lines have largely replaced the old materials. They last much longer and are easier to handle. However, it took years for different localities to make the switch to modern materials. In some places, for instance, building codes required cast-iron well into the 1980s and to this day some municipalities require galvanized pipe for supply lines.

If your home has old pipe, there's no need to rip it out. Many products are available that make it easy to connect new materials to the old. Always check local codes to see what materials and fittings are required for health and safety.

THE SUPPLY SYSTEM

Water enters your house through a pipe that connects to either a municipal water line or a private well. If your bill changes according to how much water you use, your water flows through a water meter. Near the meter you will find one or two main shutoffs.

From there, water travels to the water heater. Water from a private well goes to a pressure tank before going to the heater.

From the water heater, a pair of water lines—one hot and one cold—branch out through the house to serve the various fixtures (toilets, tubs, sinks, showers) and water-using appliances (dishwashers, washing machines, heating system boilers).

These supply lines are always under pressure; if one is opened or a break occurs, water will shoot out until it is shut off in some way. That is why modern homes have stop (or shutoff) valves for every fixture and appliance. If your home is not equipped with stop valves, plan to install them. They make maintenance and repairs more convenient and more than pay for themselves should a serious break in the system occur.

Older homes have plumbing systems that use galvanized pipe, which corrodes over time, leading to low water pressure and leaks. The builders of newer homes use copper supply lines, and in some places plastic lines, both of which last much longer.

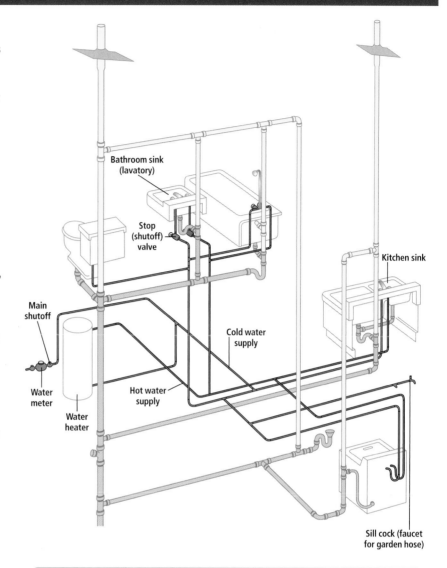

Bathroom sink (lavatory)

Stop (shutoff) valve

Main shutoff

Water meter

Water heater

Cold water supply

Hot water supply

Kitchen sink

Sill cock (faucet for garden hose)

SUPPLY SYSTEM PROBLEM SOLVER

For answers to these problems and questions	See pages
Burst or leaking pipes	24–25
Installing stop valves	26
Installing new supply lines	98
Noisy pipes	21
Preventing frozen pipes	22–23
Removing and installing pipes and fittings	142–155
Repairing faucets	27–45
Types, sizes of pipes and fittings	132–137
Water filters	117–118
Water heaters	52–61

THE DRAIN SYSTEM

The drain system uses gravity to rid the house of liquid and solid waste. It also guards against foul-smelling and potentially harmful gases entering the house from the municipal drain system or the septic field.

All fixtures, with the exception of the toilet, empty into a trap (toilets have built-in traps). A trap is a curved section of drainpipe that holds enough standing water to make an airtight seal. The seal prevents sewer gases from backing up and leaking into the home. Each time a fixture is used, the old water in the trap is forced down the line and replaced with new water.

After leaving the trap, drain water travels through pipes sloped at no less than ¼ inch per foot toward a large, vertical pipe (called a waste stack or a soil pipe) that carries water below the floor. There it takes a bend and proceeds out to a municipal sewer line or a private septic system. A cleanout provides a place where you can insert an auger to clear the line. Traps serve the same function.

Drainpipes come in various diameters, depending on what they will be used for: 1¼-inch pipe for bathroom sinks, 1½-inch for kitchen sinks and bathtubs, and 3- or 4-inch for toilets. The stack is usually a 4-inch pipe. Older homes use cast-iron pipe for the stacks and galvanized pipe for other drain lines. New homes use plastic, and occasionally copper, for stacks and drains.

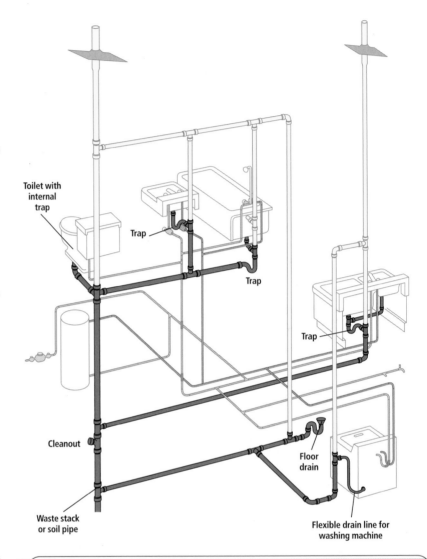

Toilet with internal trap

Trap

Trap

Trap

Cleanout

Floor drain

Waste stack or soil pipe

Flexible drain line for washing machine

DRAIN SYSTEM PROBLEM SOLVER	
For answers to these problems and questions	See pages
Adding a plastic drain line	94
Clogged drains	66-77
Drain assemblies	77
New garbage disposer	120-121
Planning new drain lines	86-87
Tapping into drain lines	92-93
Toilets	46-51
Tying into a cast-iron drain line	95
Types of pipes and fittings	132-137
Working with plastic pipe and tubing	152-155

THE VENT SYSTEM

To flow freely, drainpipes need air. Without air, water glugs down a drain like soda from a bottle. A plumbing vent plays the same role as the second, smaller opening in a gasoline can. With the opening closed, gas pours out slowly. But once the stopper is removed, air enters the can and allows the liquid to flow freely.

The air supplied by a vent also prevents siphoning action, which might otherwise pull water out of traps and toilets and allow sewage gases to enter the house. Instead, vents carry the gases through the roof. Sewer gas, composed largely of methane, is not only smelly, it is also harmful and dangerous. Don't be tempted to install a substandard venting system, even if it means avoiding a lot of work.

A main vent is an extension of the waste stack and reaches upward through the roof. Branch vents tie into the main vent. Every plumbing fixture and appliance must be vented properly, either tying into a main vent or having a vent of its own that extends through the roof.

When installing a new fixture in a new location (not just replacing an existing fixture), venting is often the most difficult problem to overcome. Local codes require that venting meets specific dimension requirements. Research these requirements before you begin planning. Vent pipes are made of the same materials as drainpipes, though sometimes they are smaller in diameter.

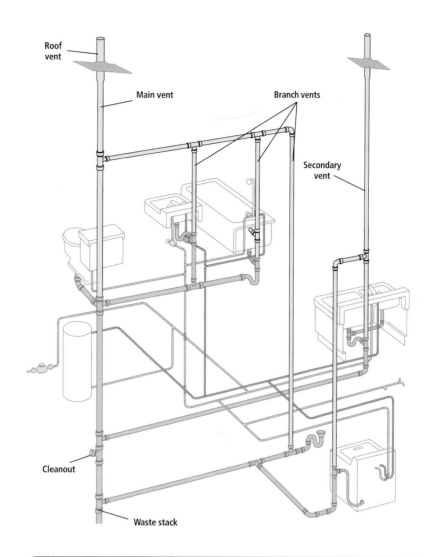

Roof vent

Main vent

Branch vents

Secondary vent

Cleanout

Waste stack

VENT SYSTEM PROBLEM SOLVER

For answers to these problems and questions	See pages
Adding a new vent	96-97
Fitting for vents	134-135
Planning drains and vents	86-89
Roof flashing for a vent	96-97
Tapping new vents into old	92-93
Tying a new plastic vent into a cast-iron vent	95
Types of pipe used for venting	132-133
Wet venting	88-89
Working with plastic pipe	152-155

Planning
FOR PLUMBING

For most people, the prospect of completing a plumbing repair or upgrade takes a backseat to virtually all other home remodeling projects. Yet plumbing may be the most important of all creature comforts. The supply plumbing provides water, and the drain system removes waste. As you review some of the inspirational photos on this and the following pages, the plumbing necessary to make these rooms work probably won't enter your thoughts, but it is the hardworking pipes and fittings that make the glamour of fixtures and appliances useful.

KITCHEN CONVENIENCE

Icemaker-equipped refrigerators provide the luxury and convenience of a cold glass of water with or without ice. Turn to page 119 to learn how to tap into a water line and connect the icemaker.

FULL-SERVICE LAUNDRY

Installing a laundry sink adds to the functionality of the laundry room, providing a place to soak out those tough stains. This vanity-style cabinet stores detergent and supplies out of sight.

STREAMLINED ELEGANCE

A pedestal sink conserves valuable space in a small bathroom. If replacing an existing vanity, you may need to move water supply lines and drainpipe (page 103).

A PLACE TO UNWIND

The whirlpool tub provides a sense of elegance and transforms the bathroom into a sanctuary of private relaxation. The bath's jetted mix of air and water massages away the muscle tension of the day. A challenging project for the average do-it-yourselfer, installation requires carpentry, plumbing, and tiling skills (pages 109–112).

UPGRADE A MASTER BATH

Faucets offer a compelling range of styles, colors, and materials to accommodate personal aesthetics and tastes of design. These single-control faucets combine a clean look with ease of operation, which frees up additional countertop space for the vanity. Rimmed oval sinks provide separate islands of usage and elongate the look of the new vanity. Pages 86–87 help you plan the installation of fixtures and sinks. You can install the faucets (pages 42–45), rimmed sinks (pages 99–100), and vanity (page 102) following the step-by-step instructions in this book.

SINGLE-HANDED CONTROL

A built-in sprayer is an option on many newer single-control kitchen faucets. Pull the head of the fixture and the flexible hose allows you to fill pitchers, spray vegetables, or clean the sink.

MULTIPLE-COOK DESIGN

Consider how you will work in an upgraded kitchen when planning new plumbing fixtures. Here a single-bowl prep sink in the island serves the cooking zone. The main sink and dishwasher occupy a cleanup area on the window wall.

TOILET DESIGN

Two-piece toilets feature the traditional design of a separate tank and bowl. The tank is mounted to the bowl with several bolts and rubber washers that create a flexible seal. Whether you prefer contemporary or nostalgic, you'll find a toilet to suit your decorative needs.

ACCESSORIZE WITH A HAND SPRAYER

The bath hand sprayer makes the perfect accessory to a bath design that comes without its partner, a shower. Available in a variety of finishes and styles to accent the fixtures in the bath, hand sprayers provide the functional qualities of the shower with the benefit of easy installation.

RETRO REMODEL
Today's style options allow you to make over
your old bath yet retain its charming retro look.
See page 103 to install pedestal sinks and
pages 42–45 to install faucets. Your new bath
will be modern only in convenience.

Minor
IMPROVEMENTS AND REPAIRS

Is your house suffering from a leaking faucet, a toilet that runs and runs, or a water heater that goes cold in the middle of your shower? Oh, the joys of home ownership! The cost of hiring a professional to fix everything may make you want to move back in with your parents. But don't fret. You can do these repairs yourself. The following pages take the mystery out of plumbing projects and show you the step-by-step processes of minor improvements and repairs. So set down the phone and put the money back in your wallet. Let this chapter provide you with all the skills and confidence you need.

INNOVATIVE, STYLISH FAUCETS

New faucet designs make replacement a much more appealing option over repair. Exciting developments include high-arc spouts, ergonomically designed pullout spouts, and easy-to-operate single-handled levers. Attractive shapes and durable finishes abound.

REPLACE THE OLD TOILET

The new low-water consumption toilets both look and work better than ever. Improvements in engineering have corrected the clogging problems that made earlier models undesirable.

BATH REVIVAL

Bath spouts have transcended the simple chrome spout of your parents' home. A variety of styles and finishes allows you to match fixtures and the decor of your bathroom. From stylish modern with innovative, fresh water delivery to the classic look, they are not only functional but add to the aesthetics of the space.

In older homes, the shutoff valves for the main line often are worn and rusted. If you have a shutoff up-line (closer to the water main) from the valve, you can easily shut off the water and replace the valve. If not, your options are to live with a less-than-perfect valve or pay the water company to shut off your water while you change valves.

If the shutoff valve handle breaks off in such a way that you cannot easily replace it, use pliers or a pipe wrench to turn the valve off and on. If you want to make sure all household members can turn off the water in case of an emergency, however, you'll eventually have to replace the valve.

These valves also commonly leak from the packing nut when the valve is open or closed. To fix it, tighten the nut gently. Don't apply too much force when tightening, or the valve may crack. If a slow drip continues, place a bucket under it and watch it for a day or two—sometimes the leak stops on its own.

If not, you will need to repack the valve. Make sure the valve is shut off. Turn it clockwise until it tightens. Unscrew the screw at the top and remove the handle. Loosen and remove the packing nut. Apply strand packing or a packing washer (see page 29) and reinstall the packing nut.

You can purchase valves that screw onto galvanized pipe or brass adapters, or solder onto copper lines.

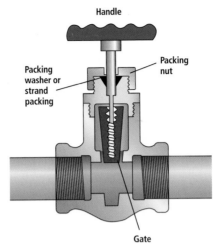

GATE VALVE.

This style of valve, commonly found in older houses, is not as reliable as a globe or ball valve, so replace it if you have the opportunity. A wedge-shaped brass "gate" screws up and down to control water flow. If it does not fully stop water flow, it cannot be repaired. To repair a leak around the handle, replace the packing washer or strand packing.

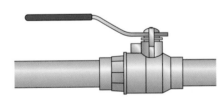

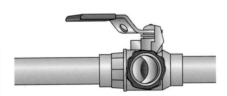

BALL VALVE.

These cost more than the other valves but are more reliable and are easy to shut off quickly. The lever rotates a ball-like gate pierced by an opening. The gate pivots to control the flow of water.

GLOBE VALVE.

This works in much the same way stem faucets do (see page 27). It is more reliable and more easily repaired than a gate valve. If it does not fully stop water and you can shut off the flow prior to the valve, replace the stem washer. To repair a leak around the handle, replace the packing washer.

AVOID CLOGGING FAUCETS

Over the years, rust, lime, and sediment deposits build up inside pipes. Whenever you shut off water and turn it back on in a house that has old galvanized pipe, these deposits loosen and flow through the pipes. After turning off the main valve, take the time to remove aerators from the faucets and let the water run for a couple of minutes to flush out the gunk.

QUIETING NOISY PIPES

Sudden changes in water pressure can cause pipes to vibrate, causing noise when they hit the house's framing. This page tells you what causes the noise and what you can do about it.

Water hammer is the most common pipe noise. It results from a sudden stop in the flow of water, as when you turn off a faucet. The abrupt halting of water flow creates a shock wave in the pipes, causing them to vibrate and hit against framing members.

A ticking noise can be traced to a hot water pipe that was cool, then suddenly is heated by water running through it. Pipe insulation dampens the noise. Chattering or moaning sounds may be caused by water pressure that is too high. If this is a persistent problem, call a professional to check the pressure.

DON'T BLAME PIPES

- A machine-gun rattle, an annoying sound sometimes heard when you barely open a faucet, usually is caused by a defective seat washer.

- Do pipes pound only when you run the dishwasher? An aging pump valve creates the same rattle as a defective seat washer. Replace the pump.

YOU'LL NEED

TIME: Several hours to install an air chamber or to cushion pipes.

SKILLS: Connecting pipes.

TOOLS: Knife and hammer for pipe insulation, basic plumbing tools for adding an air chamber.

CUSHION HAMMERING PIPES.

Have a helper do whatever it is that causes the noise (flush the toilet or run hot water, for instance) while you search for the source of the noise. Once you find the source, see if one of the pipes has been knocking against or rubbing a joist. Cushion the pipe at the trouble spot with pieces of foam pipe insulation (*left*), or use sound-insulating pipe hangers (*right*).

INSTALL AN AIR CHAMBER.

To eliminate pipe noises, install air chambers at accessible points in your supply lines. Chambers provide a pocket of air for water to bump against. Cut the pipe, install a tee (see pages 142–144), and solder the chamber in place. For galvanized pipe, cut the pipe and, with nipples and a union, install a tee that allows you to attach the chamber (see pages 150–151).

PREVENTING FREEZE-UPS

Ice-cold tap water may taste refreshing, but it also can be a chilling sign that your plumbing is in trouble. Frozen pipes that have burst are difficult and expensive to fix, so take precautions if you suspect that your system will not survive the coldest days of the year. Pipes placed near an exterior wall in new homes are as prone to freezing as pipes in poorly insulated older homes. Often the best solution is to insulate the wall or ceiling that contains the pipes, which helps keep a home warm and protects pipes at the same time. This page shows some additional ways to prevent plumbing freeze-ups.

YOU'LL NEED

TIME: About three hours to prepare the average home.

SKILLS: Beginner carpentry and plumbing skills.

TOOLS: Knife, flashlight.

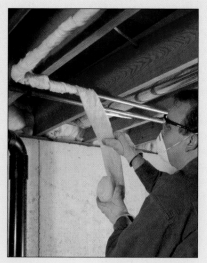

INSULATE THE PIPES.

Insulation prevents freeze-ups, as long as every square inch of pipe—including connections—is protected. Pipe jacketing comes in standard lengths that can be cut with a knife and secured with electrical tape. Ordinary insulation, cut in strips and bundled around pipes, works equally well for less cost but more labor. For extremely cold walls or floors, pack the entire cavity with insulation. Also consider insulating long runs of hot water pipes, especially those that pass through unheated spaces. The added insulation conserves energy used to heat the water.

WRAP PIPES WITH HEAT TAPE.

Electric heat tape draws modest amounts of current, so it is safe and inexpensive to use. Wrap tape around the pipe and plug the tape into a receptacle. A thermostat turns the tape on and off as needed. Tape will not work during a power outage—when the protection may be most needed.

PROTECT THE SILL COCK.

Before the winter cold arrives, remove and drain garden hoses to prevent them from splitting. Shut off the water leading to the sill cock, allow it to drain, and leave it open. If there is no indoor shutoff, install one (see page 26) or install a freeze-proof sill cock—an improvement that local codes may require.

PRECAUTIONS FOR VERY COLD DAYS.

As a preventive measure on extremely cold days, slightly turn on the faucets that have vulnerable parts, letting water trickle constantly. If there is a cabinet underneath, open its doors to let room heat warm the pipes. Use a small lamp to warm pipes that run through cold areas such as a garage or closet.

WINTERIZING A HOUSE

If you're leaving a house or cabin for an extended period of time during the winter, you don't have to leave the heat on in order to avoid plumbing disasters. Instead, save money by turning off your utilities and winterizing them, a process that involves shutting off the water supply and draining the whole plumbing system. If you have a private water system, such as a well, the process is slightly more involved because you'll have to drain the holding tank and any water-treating apparatus. As a result, you'll have peace of mind that the plumbing system is safely dormant, without the expense of keeping the home fires burning.

YOU'LL NEED

TIME: About four hours to winterize an average-size house.

SKILLS: Disconnecting pipes.

TOOLS: Pipe wrench, adjustable wrench, bucket.

1 DRAIN THE SYSTEM.

Have the water department shut off the water valve outside your home, or do it yourself. Then open every faucet in the house, starting at the top of the system. Shut down and drain the water heater (see page 55). Detach drain hoses on dish and clothes washers.

2 OPEN VALVES AND UNIONS.

See if your system has a drainable valve or two—often they are near the water meter. Open the drain cock on each. Drain supply lines completely. If you find a low-lying pipe without a faucet or drain cock, open a union where two pipes join (see pages 24–25).

3 REPLACE WATER WITH ANTIFREEZE.

Flush toilets, then pour a gallon of antifreeze solution (automotive antifreeze mixed with water according to directions on the container) into the bowl. This will start a mild flushing action, though some of it will remain in the toilet's trap. Pour antifreeze solution into all fixtures with a trap: sinks, showers, bathtubs, and the washing-machine standpipe. If your house has a main house trap, fill the elbow portion with full-strength antifreeze.

HOME AGAIN

After returning to your winterized house, follow these steps, in order:

- Turn all faucets off, including the sill cock. Remove any faucet aerators and clean if necessary.

- Reconnect all disconnected pipes and close down all drainable valves.

- Turn on the main water-supply valve.

- Turn on all the faucets slowly, beginning at the sill cock. The water will spit out before resuming a normal flow.

- Replace the aerators.

FIXING LEAKS AND FROZEN PIPES

Water that escapes from a pipe can wreak havoc in your house. Even a tiny leak that is left to drip day and night soon rots away everything in its vicinity. A pipe that freezes and bursts can produce a major flood.

As soon as you spot any sign of a leak, shut off the water to take pressure off the line. Then locate exactly where the problem is. If the pipe is concealed, this may be difficult, because water can travel a long way along the outside of the pipe, a floor joist, or a subfloor. Eventually a leaking pipe must be replaced (see pages 132–155), but these emergency measures will temporarily stop the flow.

IT MAY NOT BE A LEAK ...

If a pipe appears wet all along its length, the problem may be condensation from humid air rather than leaking. Wrap the pipe with insulation to stop the condensation (see page 22).

OR IT MAY BE MORE

Sometimes an isolated leak signifies aging pipes. The galvanized pipe common to older homes tends to rust from the inside out. Once a leak appears, you can expect others to follow. If the pipes in your house have begun to deteriorate, buy a supply of pipe clamps to fit your lines.

YOU'LL NEED

TIME: An hour or so to clamp or apply epoxy to a leak.

SKILLS: No special skills needed.

TOOLS: Screwdriver, putty knife.

WRAP WITH TAPE.

For a pinhole leak, dry off the pipe and wrap it tightly with several layers of electrician's tape 6 inches on either side of the hole. This is a temporary solution. The tape should hold while you make a trip to the hardware store for a pipe clamp and rubber gasket.

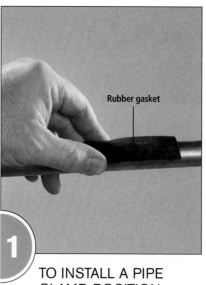

Rubber gasket

① TO INSTALL A PIPE CLAMP, POSITION THE GASKET.

The best temporary solution to a leaking pipe is a pipe clamp specially made for this purpose. A clamp seals small gashes, cracks, and pinhole leaks. As a semipermanent solution, it should last several years. Position the rubber gasket so the hole is centered under it.

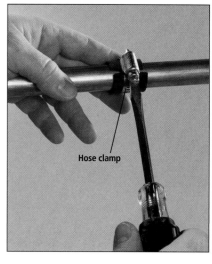

Hose clamp

APPLY A CLAMP.

An automotive hose clamp with a piece of rubber—both available at hardware stores—is a better solution (for pinhole leaks only). Wrap the rubber around the pipe and tighten the clamp. Be sure you place the clamp directly over the hole.

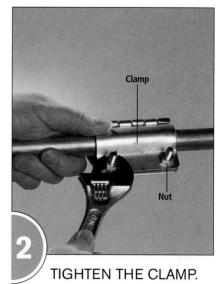

Clamp

Nut

② TIGHTEN THE CLAMP.

Assemble the clamp pieces around the gasket. Take care that the gasket does not move as you tighten all the nuts evenly, working from nut to nut until all are tight.

APPLY PLUMBER'S EPOXY AT FITTINGS.

If the leak is coming from a fitting, don't try to clamp it. Plumber's epoxy is the best solution here. Unless the leak is a real gusher, don't shut off the water. The epoxy comes in two parts. Cut a piece of each and knead them together until the color is uniform. Pack the epoxy into the connection, pushing it in with your thumb or a putty knife. Pack it until the leak stops.

SEAL A LEAKING CLEANOUT.

Drain lines are less leak-prone than supply lines. Once in a while, however, a cleanout plug seeps waste water. If so, warn everyone in the household not to use any fixtures while you work. Remove the plug (it may screw out or pull out). To reseal screw-in plugs, apply pipe-thread tape to the male threads. If it has an O-ring, replace it.

TIGHTEN JOINTS IN CAST-IRON PIPES.

Leaks that occur at the joint of cast-iron pipes are usually easy to deal with. For the hub fitting shown here, use a hammer and chisel to tamp down the soft lead that fills the joint. Don't whack the pipe: you could crack it. If yours is a no-hub system (see page 95), simply tighten the clamp to stop the leak.

TO THAW EXPOSED FROZEN PIPES, HEAT WITH A BLOW DRYER ...

Open the faucet the pipe supplies so steam can escape. If the pipe is exposed, apply heat directly with a hair dryer or a heat gun (use the lowest setting). Move the dryer or gun back and forth—don't hold it in one spot.

OR POUR HOT WATER.

Another solution for an exposed frozen pipe is to wrap a cloth around it, then pour boiling water over the cloth. Allow the water on the cloth to cool, pour hot water again, and repeat until the pipe is thawed. Be sure a faucet is open while you do this so steam can escape.

THAW CONCEALED PIPES.

If the pipes are concealed, thawing takes more time. Open a faucet. Beam a heat lamp or electric space heater at the wall that contains the pipe. Monitor closely to make sure the heat doesn't damage the wall surface.

INSTALLING STOP VALVES

Any time a water line bursts, a faucet needs repair, or a toilet needs replacing, you'll be grateful to have a stop valve in the right place. Without one of these handy devices, you will have to shut off the water to the entire house for even the most minor jobs, like changing a faucet washer. If you have an older home, plan to install stop valves under sinks and toilets.

No matter what the material or size of your pipes, there's a stop valve made to order. Copper lines use brass valves. Galvanized pipes typically use plated brass valves; plastic pipes, where allowed, use plastic valves. You can also use a transition fitting (see pages 134-135) to change material just prior to the stop. If the valve will be in view, choose a chrome finish.

To make the connection from a stop valve to a sink or toilet, you can use flexible copper or plastic line. Or throw away the nut and ferrule that come with the valve, and use the handy plastic or braided-metal flexible supply lines that screw on.

WHERE STOP VALVES ARE NEEDED.

To determine your stop valve needs, take a look at your home's plumbing fixtures. Sinks, tubs, showers, and clothes washers require two stop valves, one each on the hot and cold lines. Toilets and water heaters require only one, on the cold water line. Dishwashers need one on the hot line only.

MATCH THE VALVE WITH THE FLEXIBLE LINE

Stop valves for sinks and toilets come with either ½- or ⅜-inch outlets. Make sure your flexible line is the same size.

YOU'LL NEED

TIME: About two hours to cut a pipe, install a stop valve, and run flexible line to the fixture.

SKILLS: Cutting, connecting pipe.

TOOLS: Hacksaw, groove-joint pliers, tubing cutter, adjustable wrench, propane torch (for copper).

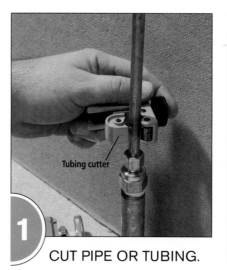

Tubing cutter

1 CUT PIPE OR TUBING.

In the example shown, the existing plumbing consists of galvanized pipe and flexible copper tubing. Shut off the water supply. Cut and remove enough tubing to make room for the valve. Leave enough supply tubing to fit the compression fitting and allow for tightening the stop valve on the steel pipe. Remove the nuts.

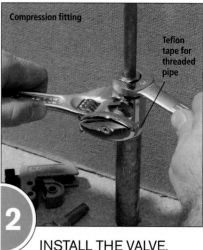

Compression fitting

Teflon tape for threaded pipe

2 INSTALL THE VALVE.

One end of the stop valve is sized to fit regular pipe; the other receives compression-fitted flexible lines. Wrap the galvanized pipe clockwise with plumber's tape and install the stop valve. Slip the copper line into the other end, and tighten the compression fitting, holding the stop valve in place with a second wrench.

IDENTIFYING STEM FAUCETS

When a faucet develops a leak—most often, a drip from the spout or a leak around the base—the problem is usually easy to fix. It's highly likely that you can purchase a repair kit for your type of faucet. Repair techniques vary from faucet to faucet, but in most cases you can easily do it yourself. When buying replacement parts, take the old unit to the store. If the faucet cannot be repaired, it's easy to replace it with a new one (see pages 42–45).

The first step is to identify the type of faucet you have. The anatomy drawings here and on pages 32, 34, 36, and 38 show the various types.

The seat-and-washer faucet, often called a compression faucet, is the most common. All stem faucets have separate hot and cold controls. In its off position, the stem compresses a flexible washer on the stem into a beveled seat located in the faucet base, stopping the flow of water. As the washer wears, you have to

apply more and more pressure to turn off the unit. That's when dripping usually begins.

Two newer faucet styles, cartridge and diaphragm, forego washers altogether. The cartridge type rotates to control flow. It uses a rubber seal and O-rings. The diaphragm faucet uses a durable diaphragm in lieu of a flexible washer.

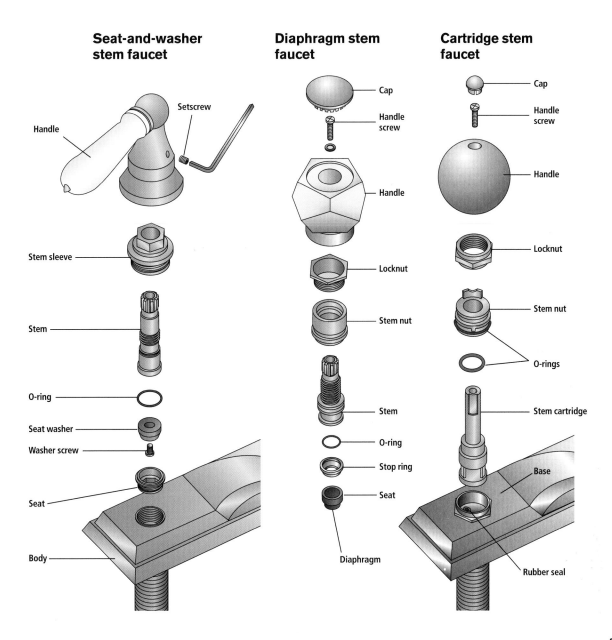

Seat-and-washer stem faucet

Handle
Setscrew
Stem sleeve
Stem
O-ring
Seat washer
Washer screw
Seat
Body

Diaphragm stem faucet

Cap
Handle screw
Handle
Locknut
Stem nut
Stem
O-ring
Stop ring
Seat
Diaphragm

Cartridge stem faucet

Cap
Handle screw
Handle
Locknut
Stem nut
O-rings
Stem cartridge
Base
Rubber seal

PULLING OUT HANDLES AND STEMS

The first step in replacing the inner workings of a stem faucet is to shut off the water supply at the nearest stop valve. Pull out the handles and stems. Take them to the store so you're sure to buy proper replacement parts. If you can identify the faucet's brand name, parts will be easier to find. Often no brand name is visible, so you'll have to take out the stem and compare it with the drawings on pages 27, 32, 34, 36, and 38.

YOU'LL NEED

TIME: About 15 minutes, unless the parts are stuck.

SKILLS: No special skills needed.

TOOLS: Screwdriver, tongue-and-groove pliers, possibly a handle puller.

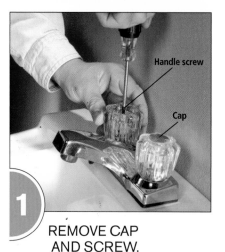

1 REMOVE CAP AND SCREW.

If the handle is round, it is probably connected to the stem with a screw from the top. You may have to pry off a cap (usually marked "H" or "C") to get to it. Some handles are attached with setscrews—see the handle on the seat-and-washer stem faucet on page 27. Remove the setscrew with an allen wrench and pull off the handle.

2 PULL OUT HANDLE AND STEM.

Usually the handle will come out if you pull it up firmly or pry it up with a screwdriver. Take care not to mar the finish. If it is stuck, use a handle puller, a tool that grips the handle from underneath and draws the handle off the stem. Once the handle is off, unscrew the stem with a wrench or pliers.

REPLACING SEAT WASHERS

The washers in seat-and-washer stem faucets often become worn. Most commonly, there is a depression running in a ring around the washer, or the washer has begun to crumble with old age.

If a washer you replaced wears out quickly, the seat is probably damaged and nicks the washer when you shut the water off. This causes the faucet to drip (see page 31 to replace a seat).

YOU'LL NEED

TIME: About 30 minutes, plus a trip to a plumbing supplier if you don't have a replacement washer.

SKILLS: No special skills needed.

TOOLS: Screwdriver.

1 REMOVE THE OLD WASHER.

Examine your washer. If it is damaged in any way, remove the washer screw and pull off the old washer. Clean away any debris or deposits from the bottom of the stem. Take the stem and old washer to the store with you.

2 INSERT A NEW WASHER.

Find a washer the exact same size and shape as the old one. If the old washer has been squashed out of shape, this may be difficult to determine, so slip the new washer onto the bottom of the stem to double-check. The right fit is snug. Replace and tighten the screw and reinstall the stem.

REPAIRING DIAPHRAGM AND CARTRIDGE STEMS

Diaphragm and cartridge stem faucets are as easy to repair as seat-and-washer stem faucets. Often the most difficult part of the job is to find the right parts. There are hundreds of O-ring sizes. To avoid mistakes, remove the stem, take it to your supplier, and show it to a salesperson.

Be sure to shut off the water supply before removing stems.

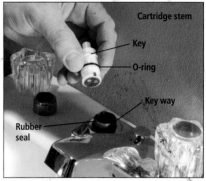

YOU'LL NEED

TIME: About one hour to remove the faucet handle, unscrew the stem, and replace parts.

SKILLS: No special skills needed.

TOOLS: Small screwdriver or a sharp-pointed tool.

REPLACE A DIAPHRAGM.

Sometimes called a top hat stem, a diaphragm stem has a diaphragm that functions much like a seat washer. To replace it, pull off the worn diaphragm and snap on a new one.

REPLACE THE O-RING, SEAL, AND SPRING.

To fix a leaky cartridge stem, replace the seal and O-rings. Remove the rubber seal from the base of the faucet with the end of a pencil; a small spring will come out as well. Remove the O-ring by hand or carefully pry it off with a sharp tool. Lubricate the new parts lightly with heatproof grease after you install them.

REPAIRING LEAKS FROM HANDLES

If the faucet leaks around the handle, you'll need to remove the stem to get at the source of the problem. The spindles of older faucets have packing wound around the top to keep water from seeping out the top. Don't be put off by this old-fashioned material; it is easy to replace, and new packing lasts for years. Newer stems have O-rings. Once you get the stem out, inspect the rest of the faucet and replace any parts that look as if they're starting to wear.

Shut off the water supply.

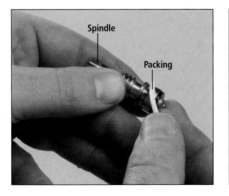

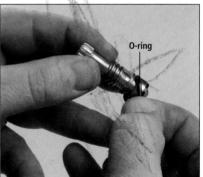

YOU'LL NEED

TIME: Fifteen minutes to repack a spindle and replace an O-ring.

SKILLS: No special skills needed.

TOOLS: None.

WRAP NEW PACKING STRING.

If your faucet has packing wound around the spindle just under the packing nut (see page 20), remove all of it and clean the spindle. Choose either plumber's tape or strand packing and wind it fairly tight. Leave just enough room to screw on the packing nut when the stem is replaced.

REPLACE THE O-RING.

Newer stems utilize an O-ring instead of packing. Simply remove the old O-ring and replace it with one that fits exactly. Lightly lubricate the O-ring with heatproof grease after you install it and before you reinstall the stem.

REPLACING AND GRINDING SEATS

If you have a leaky faucet, inspect the entire faucet to be certain you repair everything responsible for the leak. Otherwise you may implement what you think is a quick fix, only to find that the faucet still leaks.

When the spout of a stem faucet (either a seat-and-washer or a diaphragm type) leaks, inspect the seat as well as the washer or diaphragm. If the seat is pitted or scored, it is scraping the washer or diaphragm every time you turn off the faucet. It will quickly damage a new seat washer, and your faucet will leak again even if you think you fixed the problem.

If the seat is damaged, it is best to replace it, though sometimes it is hard to extract. In this case, try grinding it smooth with a special tool made for resurfacing faucet seats, called a seat grinder. A smooth seat won't damage other parts, and the faucet will no longer leak.

If you need to replace one valve seat in a two-handle faucet, go ahead and replace the other handle's valve seat as well. It's sure to start leaking soon, and replacing both now will save you time in the long run.

YOU'LL NEED

TIME: About 20 minutes to replace or grind a seat, once you have the part or tool.

SKILLS: No special skills needed, but you must work carefully.

TOOLS: Flashlight, seat wrench or seat cutter.

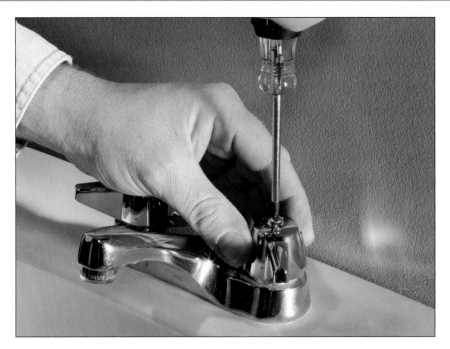

REMOVE THE HANDLE.

Shut off the water supply. Lower the sink stopper and cover it with a cloth to avoid losing loose parts down the drain. Pry off the handle cap. Remove the handle using a screwdriver.

Seat washer

INSPECT THE SEAT.

Remove the stem (see page 28) and inspect the washer or diaphragm. If it looks cut up, the likely cause is a damaged seat. Whether the washer or diaphragm looks damaged or not, examine the seat: first look at it with a flashlight, then feel it with your finger. If it appears or feels less than smooth, the washer or diaphragm will fail to seal off water when you crank down on the handle. Replace the seat or grind it smooth with a seat grinder.

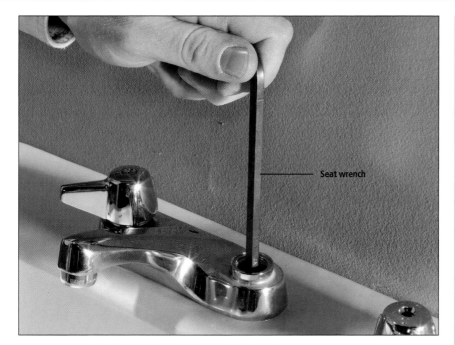

Seat wrench

REPLACE A DAMAGED SEAT.

Though it is sometimes possible to remove a seat with a screwdriver, attempting to do so is risky. You may damage the seat so badly, it cannot be removed. Instead purchase a seat wrench, which is designed to remove seats of various sizes. Insert it into the seat, push down firmly, and turn counterclockwise. Install the new seat with the same tool.

STUBBORN HANDLES

Older faucets are known to be stubborn. If you have trouble removing a faucet handle, don't think you're stuck with a leaky faucet, and worn or unattractive handles. Instead take a tip from professional plumbers and use a handle puller (page 28). Readily available at most home centers and hardware stores, a it is relatively inexpensive and is the best way to remove old, corroded components. The puller clamps over the sides and onto the bottom of the stuck handle. A threaded shaft rests on the faucet stem. You then need only to turn the shaft to pull the stuck handle off the faucet stem without damaging the handle.

Stem nut

Cutter head

1 USE A SEAT GRINDER FOR A SEAT THAT CANNOT BE REMOVED.

Purchase a seat grinder. Slip the stem nut over the shaft of the seat grinder—it helps stabilize the grinder. Select a cutter head that fits easily inside the body and is as wide as the seat.

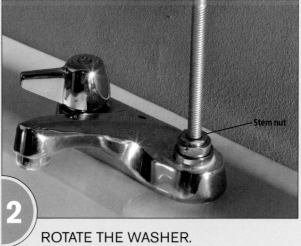

Stem nut

2 ROTATE THE WASHER.

Screw the stem nut into the faucet body to hold the shaft securely without wobbling. Push down gently and turn the handle clockwise three full rotations. Remove the grinder and inspect the seat with a flashlight. If it is not smooth, try again. When you're done, flush any debris that resulted from grinding: Either hold a rag over the opening and gently open the supply valve, or blow out the debris with compressed air. Reassemble the faucet.

Most of the faucets that work without washers use a combination of seals and O-rings to control and direct water. A cartridge faucet is one example.

In the type shown, the cartridge O-rings fit snugly against the inside of the faucet body. One O-ring forms a seal between the hot and cold supply lines. The others protect against leaks from the spout and from under the handle. On swivel-spout models, another ring protects against leaks from under the spout. Raising the handle lifts the stem so it slides upward inside the cartridge. Holes in the stem align with the openings in the cartridge in various combinations.

Other types of cartridge faucets have fewer O-rings and use other types of seals. Repair kits are available for each manufacturer and model.

When a cartridge faucet leaks, you can replace either the O-rings or the cartridge itself, if it has corroded. Because the design is simple, repairs usually don't take long. In fact, disassembly usually makes for the bulk of the work. Be sure to find an exact match for the retainer clip that holds the cartridge in the faucet.

YOU'LL NEED

TIME: About an hour, once you have the replacement parts.

SKILLS: No special skills needed.

TOOLS: Screwdriver, needle-nose and tongue-and-groove pliers.

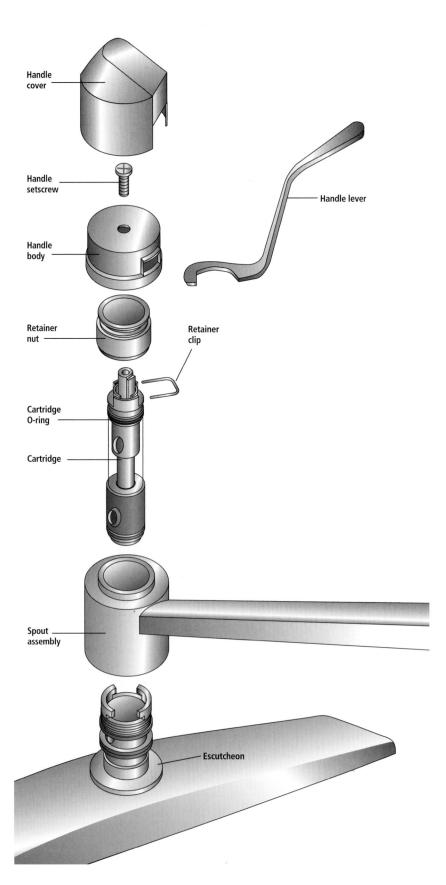

Handle cover

Handle setscrew

Handle lever

Handle body

Retainer nut

Retainer clip

Cartridge O-ring

Cartridge

Spout assembly

Escutcheon

1 REMOVE THE HANDLE HOUSING.

Shut off the water and drain the line. Cartridge faucets vary in design from model to model, but you disassemble most of them as follows: Pry off the cover that conceals the handle screw. Be careful not to crack the cover in doing so; most are made of plastic. You may need to remove an external retaining clip to get the cover off.

2 REMOVE HANDLE ASSEMBLY.

Cover the drain with a rag to avoid losing small parts. A setscrew that holds the handle in place is located beneath the handle housing. Remove the handle screw and lift off the handle body and lever. If there is no retainer nut, lift out the spout. Otherwise, proceed to Step 3.

3 REMOVE RETAINER NUT AND SPOUT.

Swivel-spout models have a retainer nut. Unscrew it, then lift it off the spout.

Some models come apart differently. Pry off the cap on top of the faucet, remove the screw, and tilt back and pull up the handle to remove it. Then remove the plastic threaded retaining ring.

4 PULL OUT THE RETAINER CLIP.

Depending on the model, you may need to lift off a cylindrical sleeve to get at the cartridge. Without the sleeve, you should be able to see the retainer clip, a metal piece that holds the cartridge in place. Use needle-nose pliers to remove the clip from its slot. Be careful not to misplace it.

5 REMOVE THE CARTRIDGE.

With pliers, lift the cartridge from the faucet body. Take note of the position of the cartridge ears (when you put the cartridge back in, its ears must face the same direction or hot and cold will be reversed). Before you replace the O-rings, give them a light coating of heatproof grease. When reassembling the faucet, tighten firmly but don't crank down hard—its plastic parts can easily crack.

BUY QUALITY REPLACEMENT PARTS

Your local hardware store or building supply center may have replacement parts that are inexpensive but a bit flimsy. As long as you are investing a fair amount of your time in making the repair, it's to your benefit to pay the relatively small extra cost to install long-lasting parts. It is usually best to buy replacement parts made by the faucet manufacturer, rather than by a general supplier that only makes replacement parts.

If you can't find the manufacturer's name on the faucet, remove the parts and take them to your supplier to ensure the right match.

REPAIRING ROTATING BALL FAUCETS

I nside a rotating ball faucet, a slotted ball sits on top of a pair of spring-loaded seals. When the handle is lowered to the "off" position, this ball, held tight against the seals by the faucet's cap, closes off the water supply.

As the handle is raised, the ball rotates in such a way that the openings align with the supply line ports. This allows water to pass through the ball and out the spout. Moving the handle to the left allows more hot water to flow out; moving it to the right draws cold water.

Most leaks are the result of a faulty ball and/or gaskets (see page 35). Seals and springs also give out and need replacement.

A leak around the handle or under the base of the spout (in swivel-spout models) indicates that the adjusting ring has loosened or the seal above the ball is worn.

Leaks under the spout result from O-ring failure. Inspect the rings that encircle the body. Also, on units that have diverter valves for a sprayer, inspect the valve O-ring. Replace them if they look worn.

CAUTION

TURN OFF SUPPLY LINES

To avoid damage to flooring and walls, turn off supply lines or the main water valve.

YOU'LL NEED

TIME: About two hours to rebuild and reassemble a faucet.

SKILLS: No special skills needed.

TOOLS: Adjustable pliers, allen wrench, wrench that comes with the rebuild kit, awl or other pointed tool.

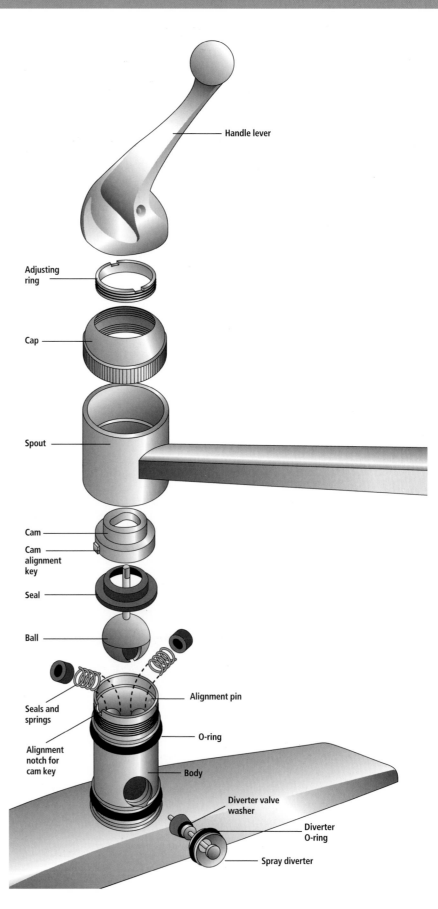

Handle lever

Adjusting ring

Cap

Spout

Cam

Cam alignment key

Seal

Ball

Seals and springs

Alignment notch for cam key

Alignment pin

O-ring

Body

Diverter valve washer

Diverter O-ring

Spray diverter

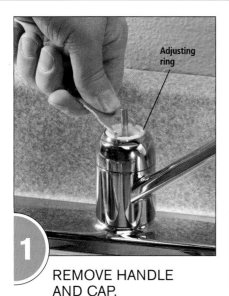

1 REMOVE HANDLE AND CAP.

Shut off the water supply and lift straight up on the handle to drain the lines. Using an allen wrench, loosen the setscrew that holds the handle in place. Loosen the adjusting ring with the wrench that came with your purchased repair kit.

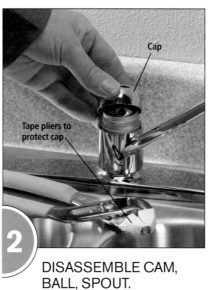

2 DISASSEMBLE CAM, BALL, SPOUT.

Unscrew the cap with cloth- or tape-covered adjustable pliers. Lift out the cam assembly, the ball, and the spout (in the case of a swivel-spout faucet). The spout fits tightly against the O-rings of the body, so it may prove stubborn. Be careful not to scratch the spout as you remove it.

3 REMOVE SEALS AND SPRINGS.

To remove worn seals and springs from the body, use a pencil to fish them out. Check for blockage at the supply inlet ports, scrape away any buildup, then insert new springs and seals.

4 REPLACE O-RINGS.

If the faucet has a swivel spout, pry the O-rings away from the body using an awl or other pointed tool. Roll the new ones down over the body until they rest in the appropriate grooves. Replace the diverter O-ring in the same way. Lightly coat the O-rings and the inside of the spout with heatproof grease.

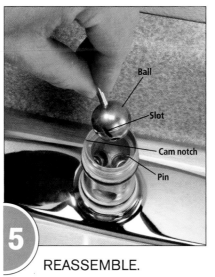

5 REASSEMBLE.

Be sure to align the slot in the side of the ball with the pin inside the body. The key on the cam assembly also fits into a corresponding notch in the body. Hand-tighten the cap and tighten the adjusting ring to create a good seal between the ball and the cam. If it leaks, tighten further.

SELECT QUALITY PARTS

You'll find repair kits of lesser and greater quality for this type of faucet. Some come with plastic balls; others have longer-lasting metal parts. If your hardware store offers the cheaper kit only, go to a plumbing supply store and ask for a kit that has longer-lasting (though more expensive) parts.

CONSIDER A COMPLETE REBUILD

When one faucet part is old enough to wear out, other parts will soon follow. If you're going to fix one part of the faucet, you might as well rebuild it completely.

REPAIRING CERAMIC DISK FAUCETS

When you raise the faucet lever of a disk faucet, the upper disk in the cartridge slides across the lower disk, allowing water to enter the mixing chamber. The higher you raise the lever, the more water enters through the inlet ports of the faucet body. Moving the lever from side to side determines whether hot or cold water, or a mixture of the two, comes out of the spout.

The disk assembly itself, generally made of a long-lasting ceramic material, rarely needs replacing. Over time, however, mineral deposits can clog the inlet ports. If this happens, disassemble the faucet and scrape away the crusty buildup.

If the faucet leaks at the base of the lever, one or more of the inlet seals on the cartridge may need replacing. (See page 37 for how to replace the seals and the cartridge.) While the faucet is dismantled, it's a smart idea to replace all the seals. If one is worn, the others don't have long to live. Before making the trip to the hardware store, get the brand name of your faucet from the faucet body (or take the disk assembly along). A repair kit with the parts you need is likely available.

YOU'LL NEED

TIME: About an hour for repairs.

SKILLS: No special skills needed.

TOOLS: Small screwdriver, groove-joint pliers.

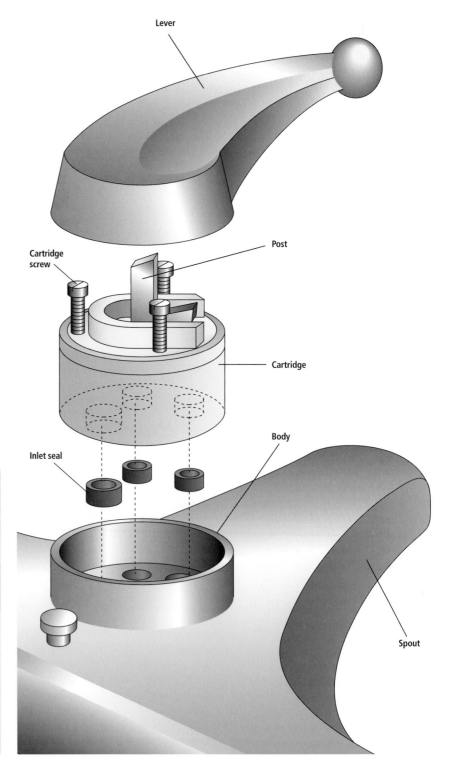

Lever

Post

Cartridge screw

Cartridge

Inlet seal

Body

Spout

1 REMOVE THE LEVER AND CAP.

Shut off the water supply. Under the lever, a setscrew holds the lever to the lever post. Use a screwdriver to unscrew the setscrew—don't try to unscrew it with a knife because you may damage it. Loosen the screw until you can raise the lever off the post. You may have to gently pry it off with a large screwdriver.

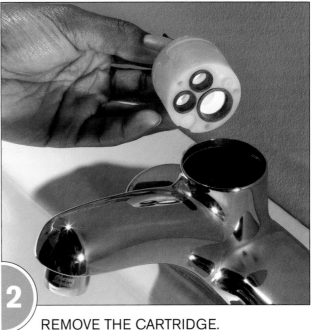

2 REMOVE THE CARTRIDGE.

Lift off or unscrew the decorative cap that covers the cartridge. Loosen the screws holding the cartridge to the faucet body and lift out the cartridge.

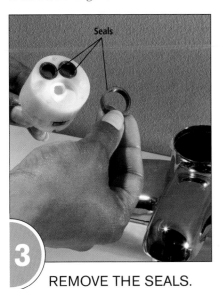

3 REMOVE THE SEALS.

You'll find a set of seals on the underside of the cartridge. Pull them out with your fingers, or carefully use a pointed tool, being careful not to scratch the cartridge.

4 CLEAN THE OPENINGS.

Check the openings for sediment buildup. If you find any, use a nonmetallic scrubber or a sponge to clean the openings.

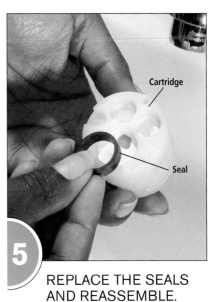

5 REPLACE THE SEALS AND REASSEMBLE.

Put the old seals back, or install replacement seals. Reassemble the faucet. Turn the water back on, and test. If the faucet continues to leak after you have cleaned the cartridge and replaced the seals, install a new cartridge.

Gasket cartridge faucets use a gasket with a group of openings at the bottom of the faucet cartridge to mix hot and cold water and direct water to the spout. Newer faucet models have ceramic cartridges; older ones have plastic.

Shut off the water supply before disassembling.

If you're trying to fix a leak from the body of the faucet, first tighten the cap by hand—do not use a wrench. If that doesn't work, disassemble the faucet and replace the two O-rings. Coat them lightly with heatproof grease.

To disassemble, pry off the cap and remove the lever screw. Lift off the lever and unscrew the housing and the retainer nut. The other parts pull out.

If the spout drips, the cartridge probably needs to be replaced. Check the threads on the retainer nut as well. If they're stripped, replace the nut.

These parts are specific to the faucet manufacturer, so take the old parts with you to the store to make sure you buy the right replacements.

If the faucet operates stiffly, debris may have built up in the cartridge. In most cases, replace the cartridge. It's more trouble to clean than it is to buy a new one.

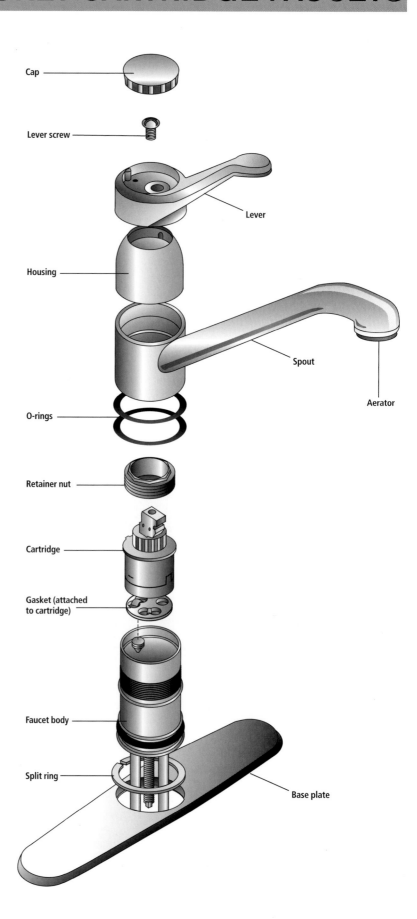

Cap

Lever screw

Lever

Housing

Spout

Aerator

O-rings

Retainer nut

Cartridge

Gasket (attached to cartridge)

Faucet body

Split ring

Base plate

YOU'LL NEED

TIME: About an hour, plus shopping time.

SKILLS: Basic plumbing skills.

TOOLS: Screwdriver, groove-joint pliers.

SEALING LEAKY BASE PLATES

If you find water in the cabinet below the sink, it could have come from three places: the supply lines, the drain, or a leak under the faucet base plate. Tightening the supply lines may solve the problem (see page 41). If the leak comes from the drain, see page 68. If neither is the cause, the sink may have a leaky base plate that allows splashed water to seep through mounting holes. If so, follow the steps on this page.

(see page 41) ... see page 68.

YOU'LL NEED

TIME: Two hours to remove, seal, and replace the faucet.

SKILLS: Basic plumbing skills.

TOOLS: Putty knife, groove-joint pliers or basin wrench.

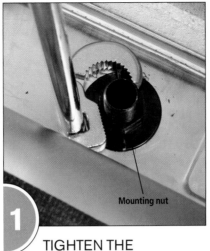

Mounting nut

1 TIGHTEN THE MOUNTING NUTS.

It may be that your faucet is not held tightly against the sink. Get under your sink in as comfortable a position as possible and tighten the mounting nuts. If you can't turn them with pliers, use a basin wrench (see page 42). If this doesn't solve the problem, try Step 2.

(see page 42)

2 LOOSEN, STUFF WITH PUTTY.

First try to fix the leak without removing the faucet. Loosen the mounting nuts enough to raise the faucet base about a half inch above the sink. Scrape out any hardened gunk. Holding the base plate just above the sink, stuff plumber's putty under it evenly. Retighten the mounting nuts. If it continues to leak, proceed to Step 3.

3 REMOVE THE FAUCET AND SCRAPE.

Shut off the water and drain the line. To entirely reseat the base plate, remove the faucet. Disconnect the supply lines, remove the mounting nuts, and pull out the faucet. Scrape any old putty away and clean the area thoroughly. Take care not to scratch the sink.

Gasket

4 REPLACE THE GASKET...

If the faucet has a gasket, throw it out and replace it with a new one. If you have trouble finding a replacement, purchase a piece of rubber of a similar thickness and make your own gasket. Use the old gasket as a pattern to cut out a new one.

Putty

OR APPLY NEW PUTTY.

Many plumbers believe putty lasts longer than gaskets, so even if your faucet has a gasket, you may want to discard it and apply putty instead. Roll a rope of putty, about $\frac{1}{4}$ inch in diameter, and apply it to the sink or to the underside of the faucet. Reinstall the faucet and check for leaks.

FIXING SPRAYERS, DIVERTERS, AND AERATORS

Sink sprayers can become obstructed at the connections, gaskets, and the nozzle. If water fails to come out of the sprayer, the problem is most likely a faulty diverter valve. You can replace either the rubber seal or the diverter. Remove the diverter and take it to your supplier to make sure you get the correct replacement.

Diverters vary in shape and location, but all work in much the same way. When water flows toward the spray outlet, the valve remains open and directs the water flow toward the spout. When you press the sprayer lever, the flow of water shifts toward the sprayer head.

If the water pressure in your faucet is low, check the aerator. Aerators develop leaks when their seals are worn, and they can become clogged.

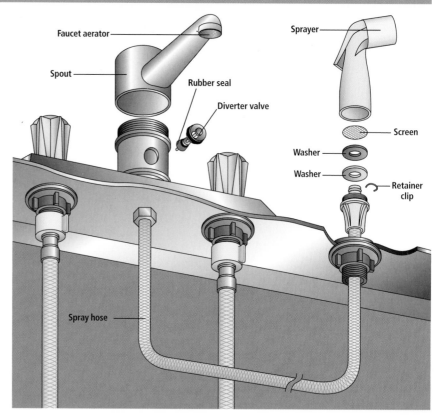

TROUBLESHOOT THE SPRAYER

Minerals may be restricting the flow of water through the sprayer. Clean the spray disk with an awl or a nail as shown below. Replace worn parts and tighten all connections.

YOU'LL NEED

TIME: One to two hours.

SKILLS: Basic plumbing skills and attention to detail.

TOOLS: Groove-joint pliers, old toothbrush, awl, or nail.

FROM DIVERTER TO SPRAYER.

To find the diverter in a typical one-handle faucet, remove the spout; it's usually located in front. If the sprayer has low or no water pressure, check the hose for kinks. A slow stream of water coupled with some water coming from the spout signals a stuck valve or a worn washer or O-ring. Replace the rubber parts or the diverter valve. Check the sprayer screen as well; it may be clogged (see below).

CLEAN THE AERATOR.

To clean out the aerator, unscrew it from the faucet spout. Disassemble it, brush all the parts clean, and soak the pieces in vinegar overnight. If it is heavily clogged, you'll need to buy a new one.

STOPPING LEAKS IN FLEXIBLE SUPPLY LINES

Three basic types of flexible supply lines are available. Plain and chrome-plated copper tubing require ferrules and nuts for connections. Flexible plastic lines have knobby ends that take the place of ferrules. Flexible supply lines— either plastic or braided stainless steel— have attached nuts at each end. Flexible lines are the easiest to use. Make sure you buy lines of an appropriate length.

YOU'LL NEED

TIME: An hour for most repairs and replacements.

SKILLS: Tightening and loosening nuts in tight places.

TOOLS: Basin wrench or groove-joint pliers, adjustable wrenches.

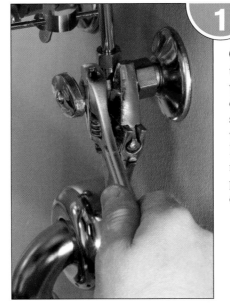

1

TIGHTEN THE NUTS.

Often the solution is as simple as tightening the nut at the point where you see a leak. Take care not to overtighten. You can crack the nut or strip the threads. Use only adjustable wrenches, not pipe wrenches. If the leak persists, loosen the nuts and recoat the threads or ferrules with plumber's tape or pipe joint compound as shown in Step 2.

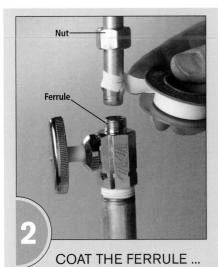

2

COAT THE FERRULE ...

Shut off the water and drain the line. If you are working with a tubing-and-ferrule arrangement, remove the nut and pull the line at least partway out. Take care not to kink it. Coat the ferrule with joint compound or wrap it with plumber's tape. Hook it back up, tighten, and test.

OR THE THREADS.

If you are working with a plastic or braided flexible line, shut off the water, unscrew the nut, and apply joint compound or plumber's tape to the male threads of the shutoff valve or the faucet. Reconnect, tighten, and test.

3

INSTALL A NEW LINE.

If these measures fail to solve your problem quickly, it could be the fault of the old line. Shut off the water and remove the old supply line. Buy a new flexible line, apply plumber's tape or joint compound to the male threads, and screw it on. Tighten both ends and test.

REPLACING A FAUCET

Thousands of styles of faucets have been made and continue to be made, with few variations in basic design. Bathroom faucets have pop-up drain assemblies, and kitchen faucets sometimes have sprayers.

Also, you have two possibilities for supply connections: A faucet may have flexible copper supply inlets in the center of the unit, as shown below right, or its inlets may be located under the hot and cold handles (below left).

The hardest part of the job is physically getting at the faucet from under the sink. Clear all rags, cleaning products, and junk from the

undersink cabinet. Remove cabinet doors if they are in the way, hook up a work light, and make your work area as comfortable as possible.

If you are installing a sink at the same time as the faucet, attach the faucet to the sink before you install the sink.

Purchase all the fixtures at once. It will save you trips back to the home center. Gather all the tools you'll use for the job. Lay all the parts and tools near the work area so whatever you're looking for is there when you need it.

Anyone can handle this job. The hardest part of replacing a faucet is usually removing the old corroded faucet. Even penetrating oil has a hard time loosening old locknuts. You may have to knock the nuts loose with a hammer and screwdriver or cut them with a hacksaw.

Place a pan, bucket, or rags below the trap. Water may remain in the lines even when turned off.

Read the label when using thread sealants such as pipe compound, plumber's putty, silicone caulk, or plumber's tape to make sure they're

compatible with the sink fixture materials. Plumber's putty dissolves rubber fittings and plastic parts. It also discolors cultured marble sinks.

>
FAUCET FANCY
Thousands of styles of faucets have been made and continue to be made. From innovative designs and cutting-edge safety features, you will be able to find the perfect faucet to complement the lavatory or kitchen.

BASIN WRENCHES

Basin wrenches make easier work of removing faucet tailpiece nuts.

The wrench has an extension that reaches up into the tight, cramped spaces where tailpiece nuts fit. The jaws of the basin wrench are self-ratcheting, so they automatically close around the nuts. The head of the wrench swivels to tighten or loosen nuts.

YOU'LL NEED

TIME: Several hours to remove an old faucet and install a new one.

SKILLS: No special skills needed, but it may take perseverance to get the old faucet out.

TOOLS: Adjustable wrenches, flashlight, basin wrench, utility knife.

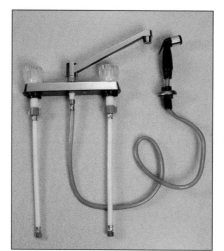

TWO-HANDLE FAUCET.

Most two-handle faucets have pre-assembled handles and valves. Each assembly has separate inlets to the hot and cold controls and an outlet for a sprayer.

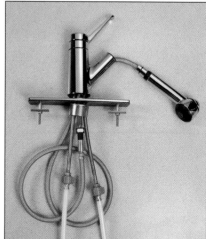

SINGLE CONTROL FAUCET.

A popular style currently is the single control faucet with center inlets and a sprayer outlet out of the center. A variety of new styles and features include ergonomic-design pullout sprayheads that eliminate the need for a sprayer.

STYLISH SINKS
Kitchen side-sink fixtures need not be strictly functional. A variety of durable finishes allow you to make a statement. Coordinate the fixture with the sink construction and pick up an accent color in the countertop, or strike a contrast.

1 DISCONNECT THE WATER SUPPLY.

Shut off the water supply to the faucets at the stop valves or the main house valve (see pages 138–139). Disconnect the supply tubes where most convenient—usually at the stop valve—using either a basin wrench or channel-type pliers. To prevent twisting and kinking copper tubing or pipe, use two wrenches, one to hold the valve or fitting and the other to loosen the nut. If the nut is stuck, spray penetrating oil, as shown.

2 REMOVE THE MOUNTING NUTS.

To remove a two-handle faucet with separate inlets, as shown, use a basin wrench to loosen and remove the nuts that hold the faucet to the sink. To remove a single control faucet with copper inlets, you will likely need to remove either a center nut or two small nuts on either side. A basin wrench may do the trick, or you may need to use a screwdriver. If the faucet has a sprayer, disconnect that as well.

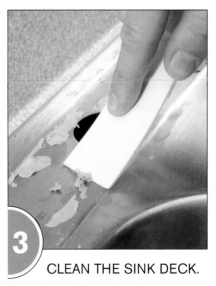

3 CLEAN THE SINK DECK.

From above, lift out the faucet. Scrape the sink deck with a plastic putty knife, which will not scratch the surface. Clean away any remaining putty using a cloth dampened with paint thinner. If needed, use a mineral-deposit cleaner to complete the cleaning.

Replacing a faucet (continued)

④ SEAT THE FAUCET.

Insert the faucet into the sink top to test that the supply tubes fit properly through the holes. Remove the faucet and reseat it onto the sink. Some faucets have a rubber or plastic flange that seals the faucet base to the sink. Others require the application of a bead of silicone caulk or a rope of plumbers' putty. Press the faucet firmly in place and check that it is centered on the sink flange.

⑤ TIGHTEN THE MOUNTING NUTS.

Have a helper hold the faucet in position while you crawl underneath to make the connections. Screw a washer and mounting nut onto each supply stem or mounting screw and tighten with a basin wrench. From above, wipe away any excess caulk or putty.

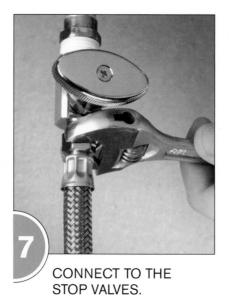

⑥ CONNECT TO INLETS.

You may choose to wrap the threads of the inlets with plumber's tape. Twist the supply tube's nut onto the inlet, tightening by hand. Then use two wrenches—one to keep the inlet from twisting—to turn the nut until it seats firmly.

⑦ CONNECT TO THE STOP VALVES.

Twist the supply tube's nut onto the stop valve, tightening by hand until snug. Use two wrenches—one on the nut and one holding the stop valve still—to tighten the nut. Turn on the water and test for leaks; you may need to tighten a nut a bit more firmly.

GETTING THE RIGHT SUPPLY TUBES

You will likely need to replace the supply tubes when you install a new faucet. When buying supply tubes, you need to get three sizes right: (1) Be sure to buy tubes made to fit a faucet, not a toilet. (2) The nut that attaches to the stop valve will be either ⅜ inch or ½ inch, depending on your stop valve. (3) The tubes must be long enough to reach the new faucet's inlets, but not so long that they will create a tangle.

OTHER MOUNTING SYSTEMS

Mounting methods vary depending on the type and make of faucet. For instance, some one-handle faucets mount via a single center mounting stud, which extends slightly beyond the threaded hole. Thread a C-shaped clip up onto the mounting stud (it fits around the hot and cold inlet tubes), then thread and tighten a nut to secure the clip against the bottom of the sink.

To install a two-handle faucet (as shown on the opposite page), connect and tighten the supply tubes to the faucet before you install it. Seat the faucet, then slip the mounting nuts up over the supply tubes and tighten them using a basin wrench.

A "widespread" faucet has three separate parts—two handles and one spout—which are each attached individually. Follow manufacturer's directions for hooking up the supply tubes for the handles and the spout.

INSTALLING A SPRAYER

1 INSTALL THE BASE.

If your sprayer does not have a plastic flange to seal it to the sink, apply a bead of silicone caulk or a rope of putty to the sprayer base. Insert the sprayer hose into the hole and press down to form a good seal.

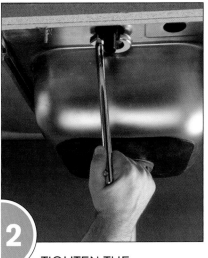

2 TIGHTEN THE MOUNTING NUT.

From below, slip on the washer, then screw on and tighten the mounting nut using a basin wrench. From above, clean away any excess caulk or putty.

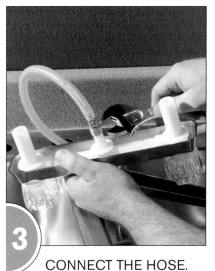

3 CONNECT THE HOSE.

Screw the sprayer hose coupling onto the faucet's hose nipple and tighten with a wrench.

CHECK OUT THE INSTALLATION

Prior to turning the water on, follow these steps to prevent unwanted surprises.

- Make sure all the nuts have been tightened firmly.

- Set the faucet handle in the "off" position: turn two-handle faucets completely off, push one-handle faucets in the down position.

- Remove the aerator or the sprayhead. Put sprayhead hoses in the sink and tie or tape them in place to prevent them from sliding out of the sink.

- Turn on the hot and cold water. Run water through the faucet for about a minute to remove debris in the lines.

- Turn off the water and install the aerator or sprayhead.

- Turn the water back on and check for leaks.

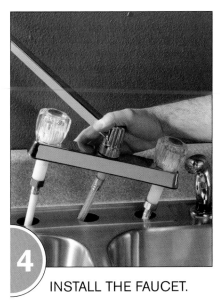

4 INSTALL THE FAUCET.

Connect and tighten the supply tubes and seat the faucet as described on the opposite page.

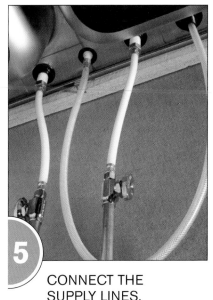

5 CONNECT THE SUPPLY LINES.

From below, make sure the sprayer's supply tube will not get tangled or caught on a stop valve when the sprayer is pulled out. Connect and tighten the supply tubing to the shutoff valves. Turn on the water supply and inspect for leaks.

Most of a toilet's mechanical action goes on inside the flush tank, which is why most common toilet problems develop there. If water continually trickles or flows into the tank and/or bowl, start with the simplest diagnosis: The float may be rising too high. This causes water to trickle down the overflow tube. If fixing that doesn't solve the problem, see if the chain is tangled or has fallen off. Then check the flapper and ballcock.

CHECK THE FLOAT FOR DAMAGE

A cracked float ball takes on water and can't rise enough to trip the ballcock. To test it, agitate the ball. A faulty ball makes a swishing sound. Unscrew a faulty float ball and replace it with a new one.

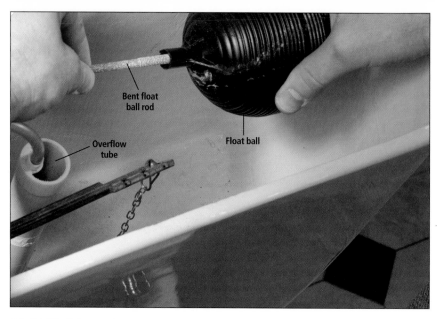

Bent float ball rod — Float ball — Overflow tube

ADJUST THE FLOAT BALL.

Remove the tank lid and check the water level. It should not pass into the overflow tube. If water is running into the tank, it will stop when you lift up the float ball. Bend the rod slightly downward to lower the float ball. With a float-cup like the one shown below right, adjust the clip.

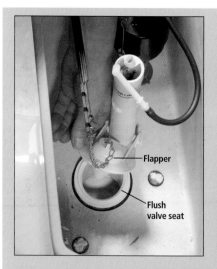

Flapper — Flush valve seat

FIX A LEAKY FLUSH VALVE SEAT.

If water continually trickles into the bowl and occasionally causes the toilet to flush weakly, the problem is probably in the flush valve. A flush valve has two parts: a flapper or a tank ball and the flush valve seat into which the flapper or ball drops to seal the bottom of the tank while it fills. Often the problem is a dirty seat.

Shut off the water to the tank and flush the toilet to get the water out. Check the tank ball or flapper. If it has gunk on it, wipe it clean and smooth, using an abrasive pad. Once it's cleaned, feel the valve seat to see if it is pitted (or corroded if it's metal). Pry out and replace a damaged flexible seat. If the damaged seat is metal, replace the entire flush valve.

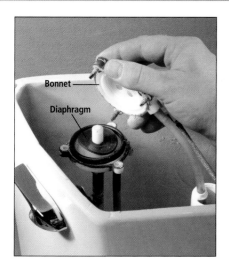

REPAIR A DIAPHRAGM BALLCOCK.

Shut off the water and flush the toilet. Remove the four screws on top of the ballcock and lift off the bonnet. Clean out deposits. Replace worn parts, including the plunger. If several parts look worn, replace the entire ballcock.

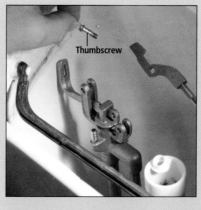
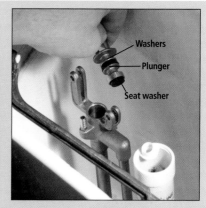

REPAIR A PLUNGER BALLCOCK.

Shut off the water and flush the toilet. This is the oldest type of ballcock, and it has many parts that can go bad. You may need to replace it with either a diaphragm or float-cup ballcock, but first try cleaning and replacing the washers (doing so might solve the problem). Remove the thumbscrews holding the float rod mechanism in place, then lift it out and set it aside. Pull up on the plunger to remove it. Typically you'll find a seat washer as well as a couple of other washers. (In very old models, you may find leather washers.) Remove and replace all of the washers, reassemble the mechanism, and turn on the water.

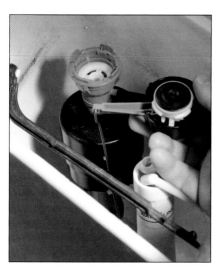

REPAIR A FLOAT-CUP BALLCOCK.

Shut off the water and flush the toilet. This is the newest and the simplest design, and it rarely causes trouble. Pry off the cap. Then to remove the bonnet, lift the lever on the float rod mechanism, pushing the mechanism down and twisting counterclockwise. Clean out gunk and replace the seal if it looks worn.

TOILET REPAIR CHART

Symptom	Cause	Repair
Water continuously trickles or runs into tank and/or bowl (tank run-on).	Water level is too high.	Adjust trip lever chain, adjust water level in tank, or replace leaky float (see page 46). Clean the flush valve under the flapper, or replace worn flapper.
	Flapper or tank ball seals improperly.	
	Ballcock is faulty.	Repair or replace ballcock.
Bowl overflows when flushed. Toilet flushes incompletely.	Trap or drain is partially clogged.	Run a toilet auger through the toilet (see page 74), or clear the drain (see page 75).
	Trap or bowl is clogged.	
Tank leaks.	Water sprays up against the lid.	Anchor the refill tube so it sprays into the overflow tube.
	Gasket between tank and bowl is faulty.	Replace the spud gasket.
	Tank is cracked.	Replace the tank.
Bowl leaks. Leak appears as a wet spot on the floor.	Wax ring is not sealing.	Pull up the toilet and replace the wax ring (see page 48).
	Bowl is cracked.	Replace the bowl.
Tank sweats—drops of water appear on the outside.	Condensation occurs due to difference in temperature between air and tank water.	Buy an insulation kit and install it inside the tank.

FIXING LEAKY TANKS AND BOWLS

A puddle of water on the floor near the toilet may be the result of condensation, or it may be a leak. On a hot, humid day, condensation drips from the cool outside of the tank or bowl may make a puddle. To rid yourself of the problem, install rigid-foam tank insulation (opposite page).

A chronic leak points to a faulty water supply connection, spud gasket, or wax ring. Tightening the hold-down bolts might solve the problem. Or, if there's a crack in the tank, patch it from the inside with silicone sealant. A cracked bowl should be replaced.

OLDER-STYLE CONNECTIONS

With some old toilets, the tank connects to the bowl with a fitting. If leaks develop at either end of the fitting, tighten the nuts. If the leak persists, take the toilet apart and replace worn parts.

YOU'LL NEED

TIME: About two hours to replace a spud gasket or wax ring.

SKILLS: No special skills, but be careful not to crack the toilet.

TOOLS: Wrenches, screwdriver, putty knife.

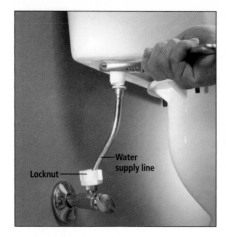

A LEAK AT THE WATER SUPPLY LINE.

First tighten the locknut that connects the water supply line. If that doesn't work, shut off the water, flush the toilet, and sponge out the water that remains in the tank. Disconnect the water supply line, remove the locknut, and replace the old beveled gasket and rubber washer with new ones.

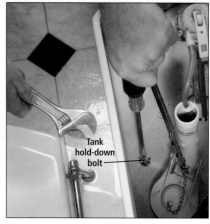

A LEAK BETWEEN THE TANK AND BOWL.

The tank hold-down bolts can loosen and produce a leak at the spud gasket. Use a screwdriver and a wrench to tighten the bolts. Do not overtighten; doing so can crack the tank. If the leak persists, you probably need to replace the gasket. Shut off the water, flush, and sponge out the tank. Detach the supply line, remove the bolts, lift off the tank, and replace the spud gasket (see pages 50–51).

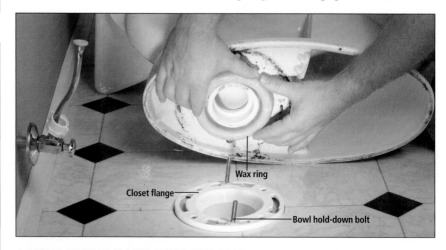

A LEAK AT THE BASE OF THE BOWL.

If the bowl is cracked, you'll have to replace it. If the bowl is sound, gently tighten the hold-down bolts (see page 50). If that doesn't stop the leak, replace the wax ring. Shut off the water, flush the toilet, and sponge out remaining water. Disconnect the water supply line and remove the nuts on the hold-down bolts. Lift out the toilet. Scrape away the old wax ring and old putty on the bottom of the bowl. Press a new wax ring in place according to the manufacturer's directions. Reinstall the toilet (see pages 50–51).

FIXING A SWEATING TANK

When the humid weather of summer hits some areas of the country, condensation can form on the outside of the toilet tank. You don't have to put up with the tank sweating in the sweltering heat. Insulating the tank solves the condensation problem. You can buy a kit from your local home center or hardware store to insulate the tank and stop it from sweating, or you can purchase the materials and do the job yourself. Before you dive into the project, plan ahead. You will not be able to use the toilet overnight while the mastic dries.

KEEP TOILETS IN GOOD SHAPE

You don't need to put up with a sweating toilet, even in the hottest weather. Follow the steps on this page for a simple solution to a common summertime problem.

YOU'LL NEED

TIME: 20 minutes to an hour.

SKILLS: Measuring, cutting, applying mastic.

TOOLS: Pencil, straightedge, scissors, utility knife.

1 PREPARE THE SITE.

Gather your materials, including polystyrene foam. Next find the shut off valve to the toilet. You'll typically find a shutoff below the tank and behind the bowl. Turn the valve to the off position. If there is no stop valve, you'll need to shut the water off at the main shutoff (see page 20). Since the water will be off and you will be working in the area, now is a good time to install a stop valve for future repairs (see page 26). Remove all the water from the tank. Use a sponge and bucket to begin; use a towel to dry the tank.

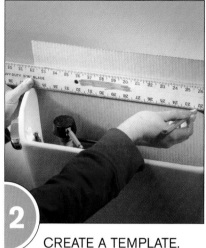

2 CREATE A TEMPLATE.

Place a piece of paper over the inside of one of the tank walls. The paper should be large enough to completely cover one side. Mark the edges of the sidewall with a pencil. Remove the paper and redraw the lines with a straightedge. Cut along the lines to create the template. Repeat this process for the other tank walls.

Using your template, cut out each piece of polystyrene foam. Secure the template to the foam so you get a precise cut. You want to create a tight fit so water will not seep behind the foam pieces.

3 APPLY MASTIC TO BACK OF SHEET.

Apply a bead of waterproof mastic to one side of a foam insulating sheet. Press the panel into place against the back wall of the tank. Repeat the process for the front and each side of the tank. Let the mastic dry overnight before refilling the tank.

REPLACING A TOILET

eplacing a toilet is surprisingly easy. Problems arise if the closet flange isn't at the floor surface (see box below) or if the floor isn't level (shim the toilet after you set it on the hold-down bolts).

Toilets are ceramic, so you must work carefully. A toilet will crack if hit hard or if a nut is overtightened. Most toilets sold today have drains that are centered 12 inches from the back wall. Measure yours from the wall to the hold-down bolt. If it's centered 10 inches from the wall, buy a 10-inch toilet or install a special offset closet flange. If you need to run supply and drain lines for a new installation, see pages 93–95.

IF THE FLANGE IS LOW

If your bathroom has a new layer of flooring, the closet flange often will end up below the floor surface. In that case, a standard wax ring may not be thick enough to seal the toilet bowl to the flange. You can extend the ring upward with a special flange extender (see page 51) or double the wax ring. Place a wax ring without a plastic flange on the toilet, then place a flanged ring on top of it.

YOU'LL NEED

TIME: Three hours to remove an old toilet and install a new one.

SKILLS: No special skills needed; be sure to work carefully.

TOOLS: Wrenches, screwdriver, hacksaw, groove-joint pliers, putty knife.

1 REMOVE THE OLD TOILET.

Shut off the water. Flush the toilet and remove remaining water with a sponge. Disconnect the water supply line and unscrew the hold-down nuts, which are often rusted tight. If penetrating oil fails to loosen them, cut the nuts with a hacksaw. Lift the toilet out.

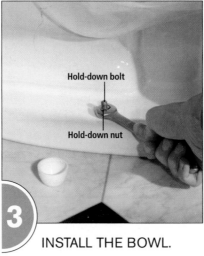

2 PREPARE THE NEW TOILET BOWL.

Carefully remove the new toilet bowl from its container and turn it upside down on a cushioned surface, such as a throw rug or folded drop cloth. Run a rope of plumber's putty around the perimeter of the bowl's base and fit a wax ring (sold separately) over the outlet opening.

3 INSTALL THE BOWL.

Return the bowl to its upright position and gently set it in place on top of the closet flange. Make sure the hold-down bolts align with the holes in the base. Press down on the bowl with both hands, and align it. Slip a metal washer and a nut over each bolt and tighten slowly. Don't overtighten—you could crack the bowl.

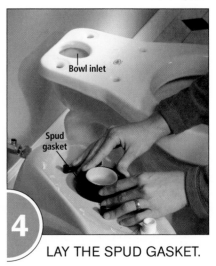

4 LAY THE SPUD GASKET.

Lay the spud gasket, beveled side down, over the bowl inlet opening. This forms the seal between the tank and the bowl. Or if you have the older-style connectors shown on page 48, slip the spud gasket onto the threaded tailpiece located at the bottom of the tank.

5 INSTALL THE TANK.

Gently lower the tank onto the bowl, aligning the tank holes with those toward the rear of the bowl. Secure the tank to the bowl with the hold-down bolts, washers, and nuts provided with the toilet. Be sure the rubber washer goes inside the tank under the bolt. Do not overtighten.

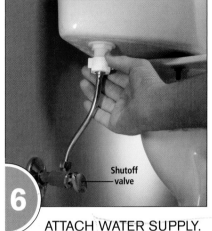

Shutoff valve

6 ATTACH WATER SUPPLY.

To complete the installation, hook up the water supply line. The easiest way is to use a flexible plastic or chrome-braided supply line. Or use chrome-finished flexible copper tubing and compression fittings (see pages 147–148). Take care not to kink the tubing.

WATER-SAVING TOILETS

In most localities, toilets that use only 1.6 gallons of water are required for new installations. These reduce water consumption, and save money, but they do not flush strongly. They differ from standard models in that they have a smaller tank or a mechanism that restricts the amount of water that enters the tank.

Don't buy a new toilet simply to save money in water use. You can reduce an old toilet's consumption by simply setting a brick into the tank or by bending the float ball's rod so the ball sits lower in the tank. Most people don't mind the reduced flushing power of new models, but if it's a problem for you, get a pressure-assisted toilet.

Extending the flange

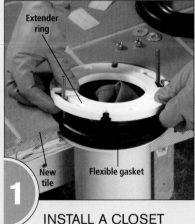

Extender ring

New tile

Flexible gasket

Flexible gasket

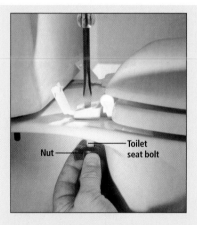

Nut

Toilet seat bolt

1 INSTALL A CLOSET FLANGE EXTENDER.

If your floor surface is more than half an inch above the closet flange (it will be if you install new ceramic tile, for example), you must extend the flange so it's flush with the floor. A closet flange extender with flexible gaskets and a plastic extender ring make up the difference. Clean off old wax, insert new bolts, and slip on a flexible gasket and the extender ring.

2 MAKE A WAXLESS SEAL.

The closet flange extender must fit flush with the surface of your new flooring. (If not, add an additional extender ring.) Add the second flexible gasket. This gasket takes the place of the wax ring. Most kits also include handy plastic shims for leveling the toilet once it's placed on the hold-down bolts. See page 50 for completing the bowl installation.

INSTALL A TOILET SEAT.

To remove an old toilet seat, lower the seat and cover and pry up the little lids that cover the toilet seat bolts. Hold the nut from below, unscrew the bolts, and lift out the seat.

Clean out the area around the bolt holes. Then align the new seat with the holes and install the bolts. Screw nuts onto the bolts and tighten them just enough to firmly hold the seat.

Water heaters are little more than giant insulated water bottles with heating elements inside. As hot water is used, cold water enters through a dip tube. This lowers the water temperature inside the tank, causing a thermostat to call for heat. In gas units, burners beneath the water tank kick in and continue heating the water until the desired temperature is reached. Heating elements perform the same function in electric water heaters. Most water heater problems are the result of sediment buildup or rust. To help prevent this problem, open the drain valve every few months and flush out a few gallons of water. This purges rust and other buildup from the heater.

VITAL STATISTICS

The nameplate on the outside of your water heater also lists the unit's vital statistics. Look for:

- Tank Capacity: The more gallons it holds, the less chance you'll run out of hot water during a shower. A 40-gallon tank suits most households.

- R-Value: The better insulated the unit, the more efficient it will be. If yours has an R-value of less than seven, wrap the tank with insulation.

- Installation Clearances: This tells you how much room you must leave between the unit and any combustible materials.

YOU'LL NEED

TIME: Allow two hours for inspection and minor repairs.

SKILLS: No special skills needed.

TOOLS: Adjustable wrench, groove-joint pliers.

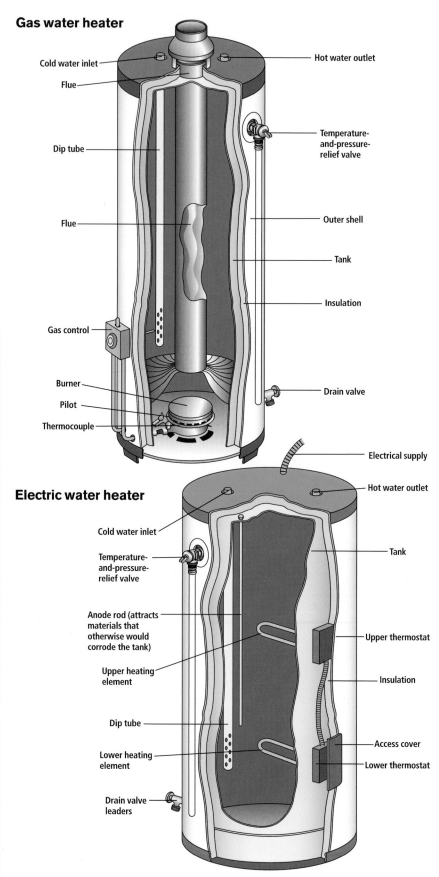

Gas water heater

Cold water inlet
Flue
Dip tube
Flue
Gas control
Burner
Pilot
Thermocouple

Hot water outlet
Temperature-and-pressure-relief valve
Outer shell
Tank
Insulation
Drain valve

Electric water heater

Electrical supply
Hot water outlet
Cold water inlet
Temperature-and-pressure-relief valve
Anode rod (attracts materials that otherwise would corrode the tank)
Upper heating element
Dip tube
Lower heating element
Drain valve leaders

Tank
Upper thermostat
Insulation
Access cover
Lower thermostat

WATER HEATER REPAIR CHART

Symptom	Cause	Repair
No hot water.	No power to the heater (electric). Pilot light out (gas).	Check circuit breaker or fuse (electric). Relight pilot; replace thermocouple if pilot does not stay lit.
Water not hot enough.	Upper element burned out (electric).	Replace upper element.
Not enough hot water, or hot water runs out quickly.	Thermostat set too low. Hot water must travel a long way to get to faucets. Sediment buildup in tank. Lower element burned out (electric). Dirt blocking burner (gas). Leaking faucets. Tank not large enough for demand.	Turn up thermostat. Insulate hot water pipes (see page 22). Drain and refill tank. Replace lower element. Clean burner, or call gas company. Repair faucets. Replace with a larger tank.
Tank makes noise.	Sediment in tank.	Drain and refill tank.
Leak from temperature-and-pressure-relief valve.	Thermostat set too high. Defective temperature-and-pressure-relief valve.	Lower thermostat setting. Replace valve.
Leak around tank base.	Tank corrosion created a leak.	Replace water heater.

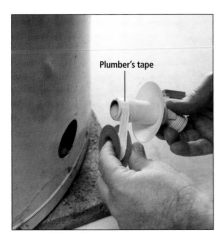

REPLACE A LEAKING DRAIN VALVE.

If your water heater's drain valve leaks, shut off the cold water stop valve, shut off the gas or the electrical current, and drain the water heater. Unscrew the faulty valve. Apply plumber's tape or pipe joint compound to the male threads of a new valve and install. Fill tank and restore power or gas.

TEST THE RELIEF VALVE.

Either on top or high on the side of the water heater, you'll find a relief valve that opens if the temperature or pressure in the tank gets too high. (Also called a T-and-P-relief valve.) Test it once a year: Pull on the handle; if water rushes out of the pipe attached to it, all is well.

REPLACE A FAULTY RELIEF VALVE.

If no water comes out, replace the relief valve. Shut off the cold water, turn off power or gas to the unit, and drain some of the water. Remove the attached drainpipe and the valve. Apply plumber's tape or pipe joint compound to the male threads when you install the new valve.

If hot water is scarce at your house, make sure the water heater's thermostat is set correctly. Drain the heater if you suspect it is filled with sediment. If you have no hot water, check the unit for power. If none of these measures solves the problem, you may need to replace the thermostats and/or heating elements. Take the element and the thermostat to a plumbing supply house or an appliance repair shop for testing. Then follow the steps here to replace what is faulty.

Electric water heaters have two thermostats and two heating elements (see page 52). To find out which pair is defective, turn on a hot water faucet. If the water gets warm but not hot, the upper thermostat and element are the culprits and must be replaced. If the water is hot for a short while, then goes cold, replace the lower element and thermostat.

CAUTION

DANGER! HIGH VOLTAGE!

Electric water heaters use 240-volt current, twice the amount found in standard receptacles. Be sure to remove the fuse or shut off the breaker at the service panel. Test wires for electricity before starting any work.

YOU'LL NEED

TIME: About two hours.

SKILLS: Making electrical connections.

TOOLS: Screwdriver, groove-joint pliers or element wrench, voltage tester.

Replacing an electric water heater thermostat

Thermostat

1 CHECK FOR POWER.

Shut off the power. Go to the main panel and turn off the circuit for the water heater. If you haven't labeled your breaker box, the circuit for an electric water heater is most likely on a 30-amp breaker. Shut off all the 30-amp breakers until you find the heater switch. Label it. Remove the screws from the heater access panel. Lift off the panel. Remove any insulation in the panel. Check for voltage using a voltage tester.

Label wires

2 REMOVE THE THERMOSTAT.

Before disconnecting all the thermostat wires, label them. This will help you reconnect the proper wire to the correct terminal of the new thermostat. Disconnect the wires from the old thermostat. Remove the mounting clip and lift it out. Always replace an old thermostat with a new thermostat of the same model.

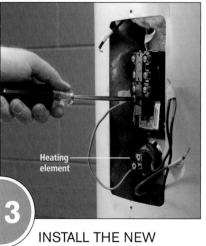

Heating element

3 INSTALL THE NEW THERMOSTAT.

To hook up the new thermostat, attach the mounting clip. Reconnect the wires to the terminals using the labels you made as a guide.

4 RESET THE POWER.

Read the manufacturer's instructions for the recommended temperature setting. Set the temperature. Make sure the tank is full. Turn the power back on at the circuit breaker. Press the red "reset" button on the thermostat. Replace insulation and reinstall the access panel.

Take no chances: Turn off the circuit breaker to the water heater and test to make sure power is off (see Step 1).

In most cases, two shutoff valves are located just above the tank. Turn them both off to keep water from flowing into the tank from either direction.

Once the repair has been made, loosened sediment will travel through the pipes and clog faucet aerators. Remove and clean the aerators for all the faucets; also clean the shower heads.

YOU'LL NEED

TIME: About two hours.

SKILLS: Making electrical connections.

TOOLS: Screwdriver, groove-joint pliers or element wrench, voltage tester.

Replacing an electric water heater element

1 **DRAIN THE TANK.**

Connect a hose to the water heater drain and run the other end to a nearby floor drain or a bucket. Open the water heater drain valve, and let the water run completely out. Shut the valve off and disconnect the hose.

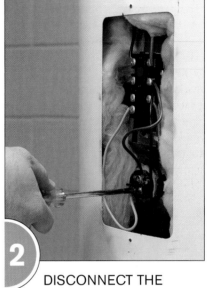

2 **DISCONNECT THE WIRES.**

Open the access panel. Loosen the terminal screws on the element and gently pull the wires away. If the bare wires are cracked, cut away the bare wire and restrip the insulation. There is no need to label the wires; they can connect to either terminal.

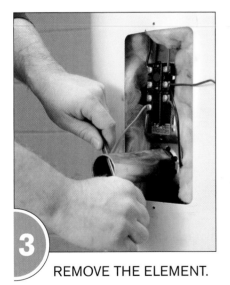

3 **REMOVE THE ELEMENT.**

Unscrew and remove the element. An element wrench makes the job of removing an element easy, but you can also use an adjustable wrench or channel-type pliers.

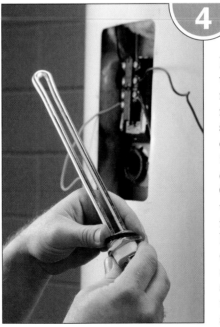

4 **INSTALL THE NEW ELEMENT.**

Buy an exact replacement element, with the same voltage and wattage ratings as the old element. Coat the new gasket with heat-resistant silicone grease. Slide the gasket over the heating element and seat it against the base. Screw the new element into the tank and tighten. Open both shutoff valves above the water heater until you hear the water flow stop. At each faucet in the house, remove the aerator. Turn on each faucet, allow the water to run for a minute to flush out debris, then shut it off. At the water heater, hook up the wires and tighten the terminal screws. Restore power to the water heater, press the "reset" button, and wait 20 minutes or so for the water to heat up. Run water in the faucets to test that the water is hot, then replace the aerators.

REPAIRING GAS WATER HEATERS

I f you suddenly lose hot water, or if your unit is not heating water efficiently, remove the access panel at the bottom of your water heater and check the pilot light. If it's not burning, relight it according to directions printed on the unit. If it won't relight, you need a new thermocouple. If a yellow rather than blue flame burns, you need to replace the thermocouple and/or clean the burner. If you smell smoke or fumes, check the flue immediately.

REGULAR MAINTENANCE FOR YOUR GAS WATER HEATER

To avoid the dangerous buildup of fumes from a faulty flue, check your flue at least once a year. Be sure it efficiently pulls fumes out of your house. To test, place a lit match near the flue. It should draw the flame up. If not, remove the flue and check for blockage. If none, call your local utility for assistance. An improperly working flue allows carbon monoxide into the house, so turn off the gas supply and electric power and open some windows to bring fresh air into the house.

Once a year, or at least whenever you replace the thermocouple, clean the burner, even if it seems fine. A clean burner burns more efficiently and extends the life of the water heater.

YOU'LL NEED

TIME: An hour or two for any of the operations on these pages.

SKILLS: Handling compression fittings on gas tubes.

TOOLS: Wrench or pliers, thin wire, small wire brush, vacuum cleaner.

Gas control knob

1 SHUT OFF GAS TO THE WATER HEATER.

At the control box, turn the top knob to the "off" position, and allow five minutes for gas in the lines to dissipate.

2 DISCONNECT TUBES.

Disconnect the three tubes that connect the burner to the control box using an adjustable wrench.

3 REMOVE THE BURNER.

Remove the burner access panel. Take care not to kink any of the tubes as you slide out the burner.

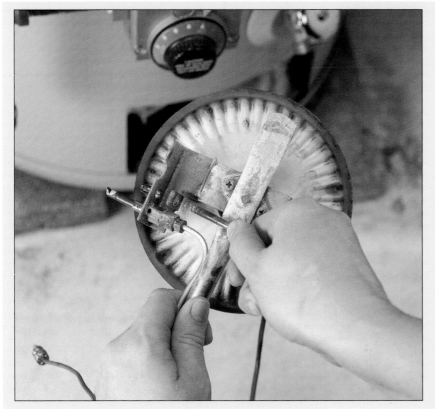

REPLACE THE THERMOCOUPLE.

If your pilot light fails to light or is not staying lit, replace the old thermocouple—a thin copper tube with a nut at one end and a solid tip at the other. Its tip may be simply pushed into a fitting, or it may be attached with a nut. Pull the thermocouple out of the bracket. At a home center or hardware store, buy an exact replacement.

Push the new thermocouple's tip into place until it seats firmly; tighten the nut, if there is one. The tip should be right next to the end of the pilot gas tube.

Return the burner unit and light the pilot (see steps 4 and 5 below). The thermocouple's tip should touch the pilot flame; if not, adjust its position.

4 INSTALL THE BURNER.

Slide the burner into the water heater. The flat end of the burner tube will fit securely into a slot in the bracket. Coil the excess thermocouple tubing in a loop 2 inches or larger. Take care not to kink the tubing. If you do, you'll have to replace it. Align the tubes and connect them to the control box using an adjustable wrench.

5 RELIGHT THE PILOT.

To relight the pilot, turn the control knob to the "pilot" position. Hold down the pilot button as you extend a fireplace match or a barbecue igniter to light the pilot. Keep the button depressed for at least 45 seconds, then release. The pilot should stay lit; if not, you may need to adjust the thermocouple's position (see above). Turn the control knob to "on." The burners should ignite.

REPLACING GAS WATER HEATERS

Though water heaters sometimes last 25 years or more, they usually give out sooner—the victims of rust and sediment. When yours fails, there's no need to call in a plumber. Though it may seem like a complicated job, installing a gas water heater involves only two or three pipe hookups, and installing an electric heater requires that you connect some wires. Removing the old unit is often the most difficult part of the job.

Before you take it out, make sure your old water heater can't be fixed. If the tank itself leaks—not the pipes—the lining has rusted and the heater must be replaced. If your heater is not producing enough hot water, it may suffer from a buildup of rust and sediment, which insulates the water from the burner and forces the heater to work more often to satisfy demand. If you drain the heater, you may be able to flush out enough sediment to make it efficient. If it still produces too little hot water, replace the unit.

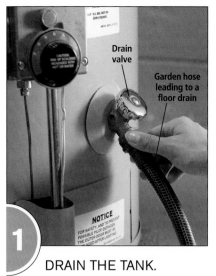

1 DRAIN THE TANK.

Shut off the main water valve to your house, and shut off the gas at the heater. Drain the water lines in your home by opening hot and cold taps in an upstairs faucet. Also open both taps positioned closest to the system's lowest point. Attach a garden hose to the water heater drain valve, open the valve, and drain the tank.

Drain valve

Garden hose leading to a floor drain

2 DISMANTLE THE FLUE.

Remove the sheet-metal screws, and dismantle enough ductwork to give yourself room to work. Keep track of which piece of ductwork goes where, and be careful not to bend it.

CAUTION

PRECAUTIONS WITH GAS

Take precautions when working with gas. If you don't have a gas shutoff near the water heater, go to your home's gas meter and shut off the gas to your house by turning the valve with a large wrench. After you turn the gas back on, be sure to relight all the pilot lights in your house.

YOU'LL NEED

TIME: Allow a day to remove the old heater and install the new.

SKILLS: Basic plumbing skills.

TOOLS: Wrenches for loosening unions or flexible fittings, garden hose, level, dolly, screwdriver.

3 DISCONNECT THE GAS LINE.

Many localities require that the gas line must be rigid pipe all the way to the water heater; others allow you to use a flexible gas line. Take apart a gas line union (as shown), or disconnect the flexible line.

CHOOSING THE RIGHT WATER HEATER

Check the nameplate on the old unit, and note its capacity. It's safe to purchase a new one of the same size, unless you have recently installed or plan to buy an appliance that consumes a lot of hot water, such as a dishwasher. Usually a 30- to 50-gallon unit is large enough for an average home.

Units designed to heat water quickly, called fast recovery units, are more expensive to buy and operate, but they handle peak demand times better. Standard units heat more slowly but are more economical to run.

If you have hard water, consider a unit with an extra anode for collecting mineral deposits (see the drawing on page 52).

4 DISCONNECT THE WATER LINES.

Mark hot and cold water lines to prevent hooking up the new heater backward. For galvanized pipe, open unions near the unit. For rigid copper, cut the pipe with a hacksaw or tubing cutter just below the shutoff valves. Make the cuts straight so you can tap into the lines easily with new soldered pipe or flexible water lines when you install the new heater. If you have flexible lines, disconnect them. Move the old unit out with an appliance dolly.

5 SET THE NEW UNIT IN PLACE.

If you need to, shim at base for plumb.

Move the new water heater into place. Position it to make your gas connection as easy as possible. Check for plumb and level, shimming if necessary. If the unit is in an area prone to dampness, purchase a tray-like base to protect it.

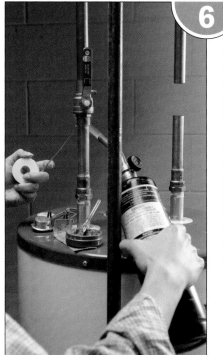

6 CONNECT THE WATER LINES.

Check code requirements for the water lines. If they're permitted, flexible copper water connectors are usually the easiest way to go. Otherwise you'll have to solder rigid copper or install galvanized pipe with a union. To save energy, install heat-saver nipples at each inlet. These temperature-sensitive in-line valves hold back water until it's needed. Follow directions, installing the cold water nipple with the arrow pointing down; the hot water nipple, with the arrow pointing up.

INSTALLING A RELIEF VALVE

You may have to purchase a temperature-and-pressure-relief valve separately. Be sure it matches the working-pressure rating of the tank, as given on the nameplate. Wrap the threads with plumber's tape, and screw in the valve—either on top or near the top on the side.

CAUTION

LIFT WITH CARE

If sediment buildup clogged your old heater, it will be extremely heavy. Enlist a helper and a good appliance dolly. Take care not to strain your back.

Replacing gas water heaters *(continued)*

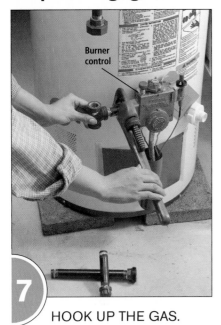

Burner control

7 HOOK UP THE GAS.

Connect a gas (black pipe) nipple to the burner control of the water heater and connect the nipple to the gas line. Be sure to install a drip leg to collect sediment and moisture from the gas line.

Flue rises ¼ inch per foot

8 INSTALL THE FLUE.

If your old flue worked well and your new water heater is the same height as the old one, you can reuse the old flue. Make sure it's clear; clean out any dust, rust, or sediment. If you replace or add to the vent, use galvanized pipe fittings that are designed for venting gas. When running a horizontal section, maintain at least a ¼-inch-per-foot rise. Insert male ends of the vent into female ends away from the water heater so the fumes will not have a chance to escape. Fasten each joint of the vent with two sheet-metal screws.

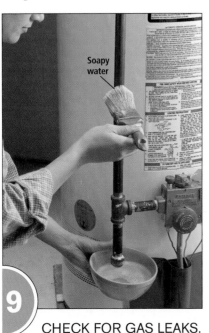

Soapy water

9 CHECK FOR GAS LEAKS.

Open the gas stop valve. Test for leaks by brushing soapy water on all the connections. Watch for bubbles. If you see any, tighten the connection. If they persist, shut off the gas, disassemble, carefully clean the threads, and start again.

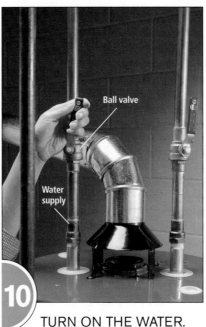

Ball valve

Water supply

10 TURN ON THE WATER.

Open the water supply valve. Open the nearest hot water faucet about halfway and allow the system to bleed. Air will come out first, then the spattering of water mixed with air. When the water flows freely, close the faucet.

11 LIGHT THE PILOT.

Open the access panel at the bottom of the tank and light the pilot according to the directions printed on the water heater. Adjust the temperature setting; water heated to not more than 120° F is best in most situations.

Installing an electric water heater is similar to installing a gas unit. The differences are that you make electrical rather than gas connections, and an electric water heater has no flue.

CAUTION

DANGER! HIGH VOLTAGE

Working with 240-volt circuits is a serious matter. Remove the fuse or turn off the circuit breaker, and check to make sure the power is off.

YOU'LL NEED

TIME: About a day.

SKILLS: Making electrical and plumbing connections.

TOOLS: Wrenches for unions or flexible fittings, garden hose for draining, level, appliance dolly, screwdriver, voltage tester.

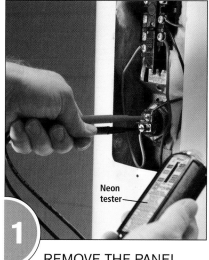

1 REMOVE THE PANEL AND TEST.

Neon tester

Shut off the power and water. Remove the access panel for the thermostat (usually behind the lower panel), push aside any insulation, and lift or remove the plastic guard. Test for current with a voltage tester to make sure the circuit is off.

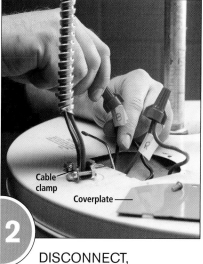

Cable clamp

Coverplate

2 DISCONNECT, MARK WIRES.

Remove the electrical coverplate at the side or the top of the unit. Disconnect the wires and mark them with pieces of tape so you'll know exactly where to attach them on the new unit. Loosen the screw on the cable clamp and carefully pull the cable out.

Complete Steps 1, 4, and 5 on pages 58–59.

Ball valve

Relief valve

3 CONNECT WATER PIPES.

Install water lines (see page 59). Supply lines can be galvanized steel pipe (see pages 150–151), rigid copper (see pages 142–145), or flexible water connectors. Install a ball valve on the supply line (see page 26). Install a relief valve and attach an outlet pipe (see page 59).

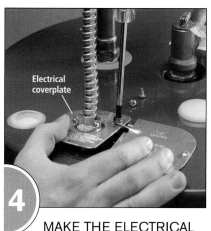

Electrical coverplate

4 MAKE THE ELECTRICAL CONNECTIONS.

Remove the electrical coverplate. Run the cable through the clamp. Connect the black and white wires with wire connectors and attach the ground wire to the ground screw. Tighten the screw on the clamp to hold the cable in place, gently push the wires inside, and replace the coverplate.

Reset button

5 SET THE THERMOSTAT.

Set the water heater to the temperature you want. Press the reset button and replace the plastic guard, insulation, and access panels. Turn the water on as shown in Step 11 on page 60.

Tub and shower controls work much the same way sink faucets do, so their repairs involve many of the same operations (except that you have to work horizontally rather than vertically). Tub and shower controls also are more complicated because in addition to mixing hot and cold water, they divert water both to the tub spout and to the showerhead. The anatomy drawings on these pages show the inner workings of common types.

Sometimes tub and shower parts are hard to get at. You may have to chip away at tiles in order to get your tools where they need to go.

If a shower control body is damaged and needs to be replaced, check the opposite side of the wall to see if there's an access panel. If so, you may be able to work from there, minimizing damage to your shower wall. Otherwise the job of replacing a shower control body means tearing up a shower wall and retiling.

Be sure to shut off the supply stop valves, built-in shutoff valves, or the main water valve before making these repairs.

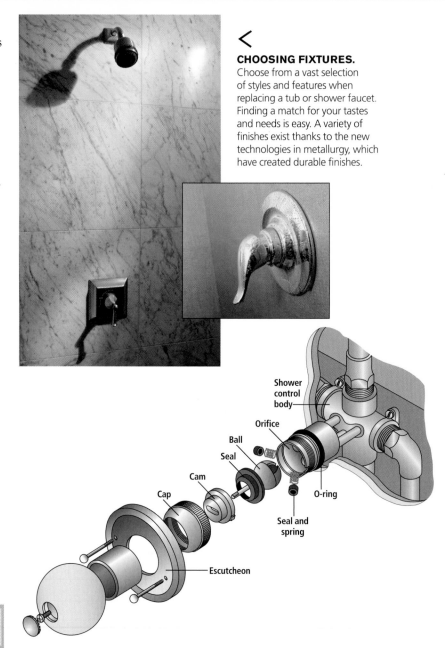

CHOOSING FIXTURES. Choose from a vast selection of styles and features when replacing a tub or shower faucet. Finding a match for your tastes and needs is easy. A variety of finishes exist thanks to the new technologies in metallurgy, which have created durable finishes.

Shower control body
Orifice
Ball
Seal
Cam
Cap
Seal and spring
O-ring
Escutcheon

ONE-HANDLE BALL CONTROL.

This type of control has seals and springs like rotating ball sink faucets, so repairs are similar to those shown on pages 34–35. As the handle is raised, the ball rotates in such a way that its openings align with the supply line ports, allowing water to pass through the ball and out the spout.

Impeded flow is usually the result of clogged orifices or worn seals. Shut off the water and remove the ball—some ball controls have setscrews that you have to remove to do this. Clean out the orifices, replace worn rubber parts and lubricate them with heatproof grease.

While you have the faucet apart, check the ball for wear and corrosion. If it's worn, replace it with a new one.

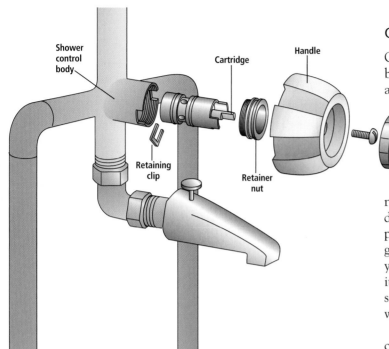

ONE-HANDLE CARTRIDGE CONTROL.

One-handle cartridge controls take many forms besides the one shown here, so use the diagram at left as a general guide. You may have to search out the location of your parts, such as the retaining clip. Parts are usually made of plastic; be careful not to crack them.

To repair a leak or impeded flow, remove the handle, unscrew the retainer nut, and pull out the cartridge. Clean away deposits and replace worn rubber or plastic parts. Lubricate all rubber parts with heatproof grease. Or replace the cartridge itself. When you remove the old cartridge, be sure to note its original position, and insert the new one the same way. If you don't, your hot and cold water will be reversed.

See pages 32–33 for more on repairing cartridge faucets.

DUAL CONTROL
This dual shower employs both a one-handle cartridge control for the rain-type showerhead, and a two-handle control for the hand shower.

Repairing tub and shower controls *(continued)*

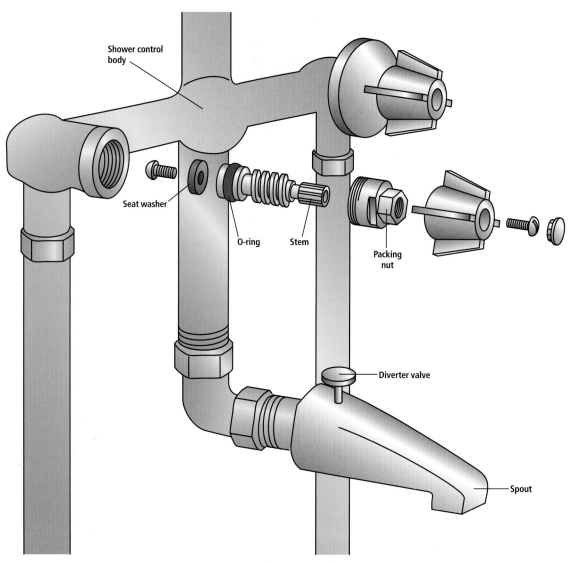

Shower control body

Seat washer

O-ring

Stem

Packing nut

Diverter valve

Spout

TWO-HANDLE CONTROL.

Two-handle controls usually contain stems with washers. Like their sink faucet counterparts, each washer presses against a seat in order to shut the water off (see pages 27–31). To stop a drip, shut off the water, and remove the stem—you may have to use a special stem wrench or a deep socket wrench, or chip away at the tiles, to get at the packing nut. Replace the washer and the seat, if necessary, the same way you would on a sink faucet (see page 28). If the diverter valve on the spout is not working properly, replace the spout.

ACHIEVE RETRO STYLE
This two-handle control complements the retro styling of this bath. Here, the diverter valve directs water to a hand shower (not shown) to rinse off after a soak in the whirlpool.

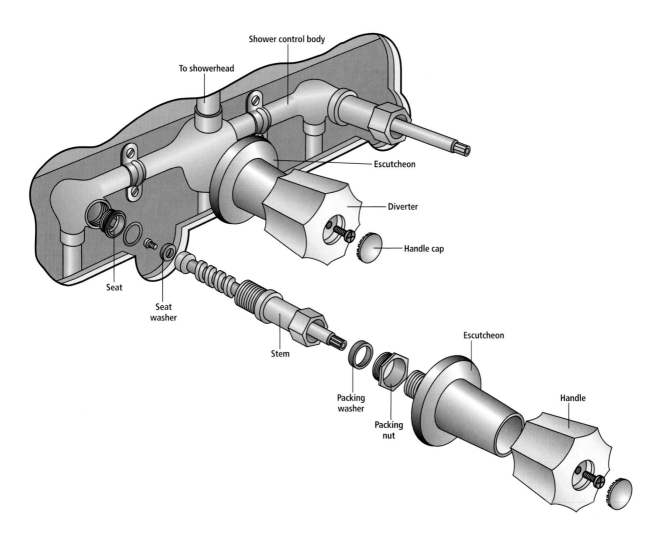

Shower control body

To showerhead

Escutcheon

Diverter

Handle cap

Seat

Seat washer

Stem

Packing washer

Packing nut

Escutcheon

Handle

>

TAKE CONTROL.
Three-handle fixtures provide a simple way to control water temperature and water flow for a tub and shower combination.

THREE-HANDLE CONTROL.

The three-handle control works like a two-handle control, but it has a central handle that controls a diverter valve. The valve directs water either up or down—out the showerhead or out the spout. If the diverter valve sticks, or if it does not completely divert water to either the showerhead or to the spout, shut off the water, and remove it just as you would a regular stem (see page 37). Take it apart, clean it, and replace any washers or O-rings (see pages 37–39). Or, replace the whole stem with a new one.

Sooner or later, every homeowner encounters a clogged drain. If you hire a professional to clear it out, you will get a better price if you call someone who specializes in clearing drains, rather than a general plumber. But it will still cost you plenty; a professional's time costs the same whether the job requires something highly specialized or something you could have done yourself.

Most clogs are due to the slow buildup of solids that sink drains aren't intended to cope with. Only toilets are plumbed to handle solid waste; sinks, tubs, and showers have drains designed to carry away water only. Hair, grease, soap, food scraps, and gunk gradually clog a drain. With a few basic tools, you can clear most clogs and get the system flowing again.

Anatomy of a sink

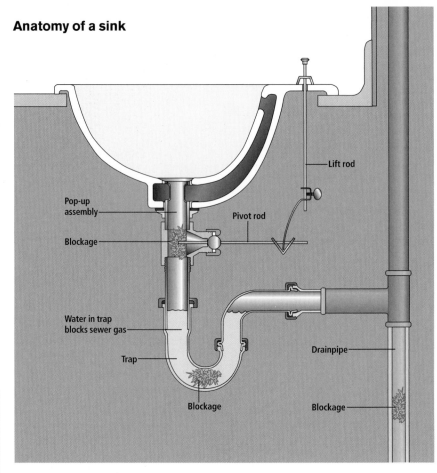

Lift rod

Pop-up assembly

Pivot rod

Blockage

Water in trap blocks sewer gas

Drainpipe

Trap

Blockage

Blockage

WHERE CLOGS HAPPEN.

The slow buildup of soapy slime inside a drainpipe—usually at a point of resistance such as a drain assembly or a sharp bend in the drain—can cause a clog. If a fixture often clogs, install a strainer to keep solids from going down the drain. You'll have to clean the strainer occasionally, but it'll be worth it.

POWER AUGERS

For extra augering power, rent or buy a power auger or an augering attachment for a drill. The drill attachment is less expensive and less sturdy than a power auger.

High-quality augers have a second cable that runs through the middle of the wound-wire augering cable. This keeps the auger cable from kinking, and it retrieves the auger cable if it should break. If your auger lacks this second cable and it breaks—a real possibility, especially if you are doing heavy-duty augering—you'll have a length of auger cable stuck in your pipe.

USING DRAIN CLEANERS

If your drain is completely stopped up and water is not moving through it at all, do not use a chemical drain cleaner. It will not help the problem, and some types will actually harden if they cannot get through, making the clog worse. Drain cleaner can damage pipes, and it might splash you when you plunge or auger the drain, injuring your skin or eyes.

If your drain is sluggish, use only nonacid drain cleaners (sodium hydroxide and copper sulfide). Wear long sleeves, gloves, and eye protection. Regular use of a drain cleaner keeps the pipes clear of hair, soap, grease, and so on.

To maintain a smooth-flowing drain, every week or so run very hot water into the drain for a minute or two. This will clear away small amounts of grease and soap and keep them from building up.

USING SIMPLE UNCLOGGING METHODS

The first step in clearing a sink clog is to figure out where the blockage might be. It could be anywhere along the three main sections of a household drain system: in the fixture drain; in the drain stack, which serves multiple fixtures; or in the main sewer line, which carries waste out of the house (see page 10). Usually the problem occurs close to a fixture, because the drainpipe and trap near a fixture are narrower than the stack and main sewer lines. Check other drains in your home. If more than one is clogged, something is stuck in a drain stack. If all drains are clogged, the problem is farther down the line, probably in the main sewer line.

PLUNGING SINKS WITH MORE THAN ONE DRAIN

Plunging a double sink requires a helper. Have him or her press a wet rag firmly into one of the drain holes while you plunge the other drain hole.

A dishwasher drains through a hose into the disposer or the sink plumbing (see page 123). Before plunging, use a C-clamp and two wood blocks to seal the drain hose and keep water from backing into the dishwasher.

YOU'LL NEED

TIME: An hour or two to perform the operations shown.

SKILLS: No special skills needed.

TOOLS: Screwdriver, auger, plunger.

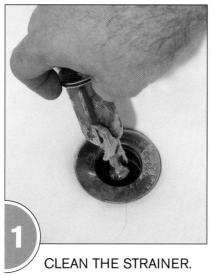

1 CLEAN THE STRAINER.

Sometimes clearing a sink is as easy as removing the strainer or stopper from the drain opening. Pull the stopper up and clear away soap, hair, food matter, or other debris that clogs the opening or dangles into the drain.

3 PLUNGE A SINK.

A plunger uses water pressure to push out obstructions and suction to bring them up. The plunger's rubber cup must seal tightly around the drain opening. Water in the sink helps create a seal; petroleum jelly around the plunger rim also helps. Stuff a rag into any openings, such as an overflow drain, then push and pull rapidly with the plunger.

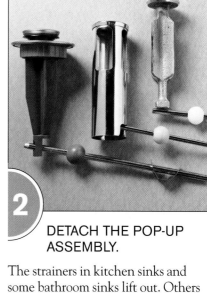

2 DETACH THE POP-UP ASSEMBLY.

The strainers in kitchen sinks and some bathroom sinks lift out. Others require a slight turn before they lift out. With some, you must pull out the pivot rod before the stopper will come out. If you want to auger the sink, you will have to remove the pivot rod (see opposite page).

4 AUGER A SINK.

If plunging fails, fit an auger down the drain. Cranking the auger handle rotates a stiff spring that bores through stubborn blockages. The auger may push a blockage through, or it may snag a blockage and pull it up and out. If none of these techniques works, see pages 68–69.

DISMANTLING FIXTURE TRAPS

When plunging doesn't clear a clog, or if you've dropped something valuable into a drain, you'll have to dismantle the trap. Before doing so, however, see if the trap has a nutlike cleanout fitting at its lowest point. If so, open it and fit the auger into the hole. If there is no cleanout, don't be discouraged. Dismantling a trap is not that difficult or time-consuming. The most difficult part of the job is getting a wrench into position if the trap is in an awkward place.

YOU'LL NEED

TIME: About an hour to dismantle and reassemble a trap.

SKILLS: Beginner plumbing skills.

TOOLS: Groove-joint pliers, plumber's tape or pipe joint compound.

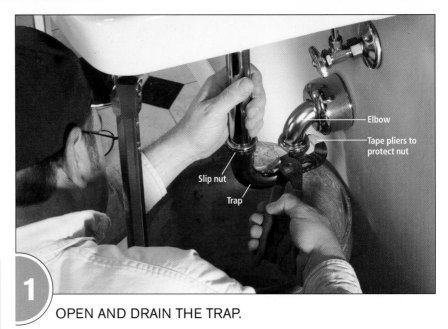

1 OPEN AND DRAIN THE TRAP.

Turn off the faucet firmly. As an extra precaution, turn off the supply valves. Position a bucket to catch the water that will spill out when you remove the trap. Loosen the slip nuts that secure the trap. Wrap electrical tape around the jaws of your wrench or pliers to protect the nuts from scratches. After a half-turn or so, you can unscrew the nuts by hand.

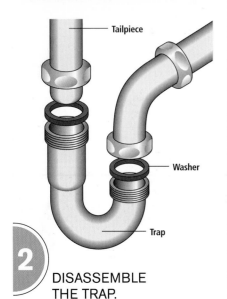

2 DISASSEMBLE THE TRAP.

The joints of the trap are made up of a nut and a flexible washer. Push them up the tailpiece and elbow to keep track of them. Dump out the water that sits in the trap.

3 CLEAN OUT THE TRAP.

Remove any gunk that has collected. Clean the inside of the trap with a small wire brush or run a piece of cloth through it. Replace washers that show signs of wear and slide the trap back into position.

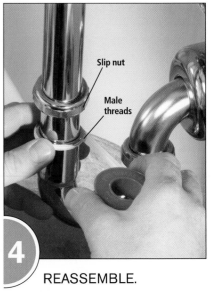

4 REASSEMBLE.

Wrap the male threads with plumber's tape or brush on joint compound. Position trap, slide washers into place, and hand-tighten the slip nuts. Use an adjustable wrench for final tightening. To test for leaks, fill the bowl, then remove the plug. Tighten the slip nut, if necessary.

AUGERING TECHNIQUES

A sewer snake, or auger, is a flexible metal rod with a spiral hook or ball attached to the end. You'll find two types of snakes: A closet auger has a bent tip made to easily slide through the trap of a toilet; a drain auger is constructed of a coiled rod or flattened metal strip. When using a sewer snake, feed it into the drainpipe until the rod encounters an obstruction. Tighten the handle and push the snake into the blockage—sometimes this is enough to clear the drainpipe. If not, twist the rod clockwise so the hook or ball snags the blockage, pull the snake back slightly, then steadily push while turning clockwise until the auger hooks the debris. Firmly push and pull the snake back and forth until the blockage is freed. The blockage may only move a bit further down the drainpipe and get stuck again. Continue to use the snake, feeding out more line while pouring water into the drainpipe from a bucket. When the blockage has been removed, reassemble the trap and flush the line. Run additional water down the drain to make sure the blockage is gone. If the blockage remains, rent a commercial power auger with a rotor, or blade bit, that chops up whatever gets in its way.

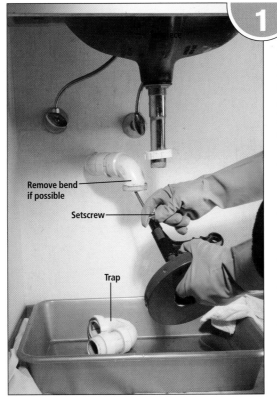

Remove bend if possible

Setscrew

Trap

CAUTION

PROTECT YOURSELF FROM CHEMICALS

Always use gloves and goggles to avoid skin contact with bacteria and chemical drain cleaners. Cleaners burn skin and damage eyes. Don't use a chemical drain cleaner before using mechanical methods.

YOU'LL NEED

TIME: Approximately one to two hours.

SKILLS: Basic plumbing skills.

TOOLS: Hand auger, snake, pliers, adjustable wrench, gloves, goggles.

1 SET UP A DROP CLOTH AND PAN.

Be prepared for a mess. Place a drop cloth and a dishpan below the drain opening and wear gloves. Remove the trap and elbow as well as the pipe that leads to the wall. Loosen the setscrew of the auger and push the auger cable into the drainpipe until you feel it meet resistance.

Give yourself 6 to 8 inches of cable to work with and tighten the setscrew. Crank the auger handle clockwise, pushing it in until the auger moves forward. Once it is past an obstruction like a bend in the pipe, you may be able to push the cable in without cranking it.

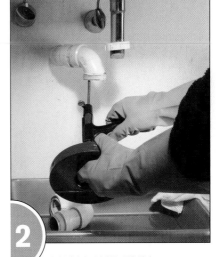

2 PUSH AND PULL.

Augers can pass through soft obstructions such as soap clogs: Use a push-and-pull motion to ream them out. If the auger comes to an obstruction and it will not crank easily, pull it out. Often the blockage will come out with it. Sometimes the auger clears the line by pushing the blockage through to a larger pipe.

If a shower stall drains sluggishly, carefully pour one to three gallons of boiling water down the drain or run the hot water for about 10 minutes. Hot water works on the elements (soap and grease) that bind a blockage.

If hot water fails, try an environmentally safe chemical drain cleaner (do not use cleaners on stopped drains). Most have a caustic soda with bauxite as their primary ingredient. Read the label carefully and follow all the safety precautions and the manufacturer's directions.

If chemical cleaners don't work, flush the drainpipes with hot water for at least 10 minutes.

If a shower drain is clogged, fill the base with an inch of water and plunge. If the drain does not respond to plunging, use a screwdriver to pry up the strainer and attempt to clear the blockage with the two methods shown here. (Some strainers have a center screw; remove it before prying up the strainer.)

YOU'LL NEED

TIME: Two hours to try both methods.

SKILLS: Basic plumbing skills.

TOOLS: Auger, screwdriver, garden hose attached to a spout, rags.

1 RUN AN AUGER.

Push an auger down the drain and through the trap. Push and pull to remove a soap clog. If the auger hits a blockage, pull out the auger. The blockage may come with it. If it doesn't, use the auger to force the clog into a larger pipe.

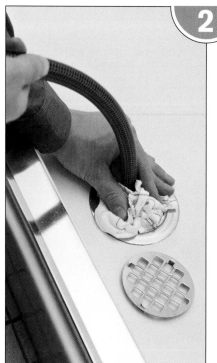

2 PUSH IN A HOSE.

If all else fails, try forcing out the blockage with a hose. Remove the strainer. Guide the hose in as far as it will easily go, and pack rags tightly around the hose at the drain opening. Hold everything in place and have a helper turn the water fully on and off a few times.

UNCLOGGING TUBS

If a bathtub drains sluggishly but is not completely stopped, pour one to three gallons of boiling water down the drain or run the hot water for about 10 minutes.

If hot water fails, try an environmentally safe chemical drain cleaner. Most have a caustic soda with bauxite as their primary ingredients. Read the label carefully, following all the manufacturer's directions and precautions. If the clog perseveres, flush the drainpipes with hot water for a minimum of 10 minutes and try plunging.

If the stubborn blockage refuses to clear, remove the strainer and work an auger through it. If you're still unable to remove or reach the blockage, you'll need to work through the overflow drain.

YOU'LL NEED

TIME: Two hours to try both methods.

SKILLS: Basic plumbing skills.

TOOLS: Plunger, auger, screwdriver.

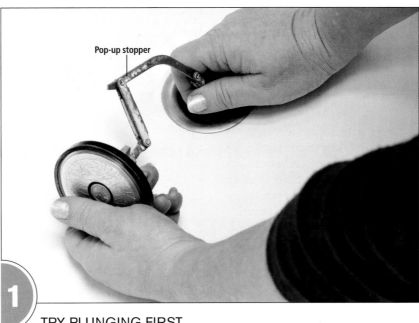

Pop-up stopper

1 TRY PLUNGING FIRST.

If your tub has a pop-up stopper, remove it before you plunge. Wiggle it to free the linkage assembly—the mechanism that connects the trap lever with the stopper mechanism. Before plunging, plug the overflow and run an inch or so of water into the tub to help seal the plunger.

2 AUGER THROUGH THE STRAINER.

If plunging fails, thread an auger through the drain. Remove the stopper and/or the trip-lever linkage. Insert the auger into the opening. This method reaches only to the tee fitting. If the clog is farther down the drain, you'll have to put the auger through the overflow tube.

3 AUGER THROUGH THE OVERFLOW.

Remove the pop-up or trip-lever assembly by unscrewing the plate and pulling out the parts (see page 77). Feed the auger down the overflow tube and through the trap. If the auger goes in a long way and the stoppage remains, find a cleanout plug on the main drain and auger there.

UNCLOGGING SINKS

To clear a sink drain, you'll need only a few basic tools. Addressing it yourself saves the expense of hiring a plumber. Just acknowledge your limitations and don't be too aggressive. You don't want to damage the drainpipe by applying too much force.

Most sink clogs happen in bathrooms. Kitchen and laundry sinks do not normally clog—hot water from appliances such as dishwashers and clothes washers purges them by removing grease and sludge. Bathroom sinks clog because of constant exposure to hair, soap, and greasy products.

Avoid reaching for a chemical product to clear a blockage. Chemical products are great for maintenance when used in moderation; but when a blockage occurs, chemical products can create more harm than good and pose a safety hazard. The caustic chemicals can actually damage the pipes. The best way to unclog a drain is mechanically.

Try carefully pouring one to three gallons of boiling water down the drain. Extremely hot water works to release the blockage by working on the elements that bind a blockage—soap and grease.

YOU'LL NEED

TIME: One to two hours.

SKILLS: Basic plumbing skills.

TOOLS: Plunger, auger, screwdriver, pipe wrenches, bucket, rags.

MAKE SURE THERE IS WATER IN THE BOWL.

Once a clog has formed, preventive measures will not work. It is time to get out the plunger. Partially fill the sink with water to cover the plunger head. If you have a double sink or an overflow opening, stuff a wet rag into the second drain or opening. This will focus the plunging pressure on the clog. Now plunge up and down vigorously, keeping the plunger sealed against the bottom of the sink. If you do not feel the water swishing back and forth or enough resistance, then air may be escaping through the second drain or overflow opening. Have a helper hold the wet rag firmly in place. Once you have broken the clog loose, run hot water through the drain to flush out the debris.

UNCLOG KITCHEN SINKS.

If the sink has a double bowl, plug one side with a wet cloth and hold it firmly in place. Run hot water into the sink, the hotter the better. If the obstruction doesn't clear, try plunging. Take care that the plug on the other side of the double bowl doesn't come loose. Apply a thick layer of petroleum jelly to the rim of the plunger before using it to create a tight seal.

If this fails, run a snake through the trap under the sink. Check the trap for a cleanout plug. If it has one, carefully remove it after placing a bucket under it first, as water will run out.

The trap is held in place by a slip nut on each end. Remove the slip nuts with a pipe wrench. Once the trap is removed, check to see if it's clogged. If the blockage is inside the trap, push an old bottlebrush around the bends of the trap to remove debris. Feed an auger into the drainpipe, if the trap is clear. You should eventually run into some resistance. Turn the snake. Feed another foot or two into the pipe, then pull it out. There should be some debris on the tip of the snake. Reassemble the trap and try running hot water through the pipe. If still clogged, try plunging again. You may need to repeat the whole process once or twice.

USING A DRAIN AUGER

If the clog is too stubborn for the plunger, it is time to try a drain auger. Generally you have two choices. You can go through the drain or you can remove the trap. Use your judgment based on where you believe the clog is located.

ACCESSING THROUGH A TRAP.

Remove the trap using a pipe wrench. Wrap tape around the jaws of the wrench to prevent the teeth of the tool from marring the surface. Remove the slip nuts holding the trap. You need direct access into the horizontal stretch of pipe. Be sure to put a bucket under the trap to catch residual water contained in the trap.

USING THE DRAIN AUGER.

Loosen the setscrew of the auger and push the auger cable in. When you feel resistance, you are probably up against the clog. Pull an extra 12–18 inches of cable out of the housing, tighten the setscrew securing the cable, and turn the crank on the auger, applying moderate force so that you push the cable into the drainpipe. When the free cable has worked into the pipe, loosen the setscrew and pull out another 12–18 inches. Continue this procedure until the cable has reached the larger vertical pipe.

FINISHING THE JOB.

Pull the cable back out, cleaning it and feeding it back into the housing as you go. If you removed the trap, replace it now. The slip nuts holding the drain in place should be tightened by hand and turned about a quarter turn with the wrench or channel locks. Do not overtighten. Once the trap is replaced, run hot water through the drain to flush it out. If water backs up, there may still be some loose debris in the line left behind by the auger. Try plunging to get rid of residual debris. Flush with hot water.

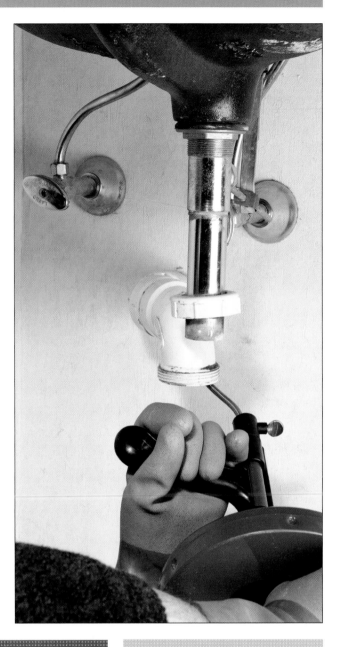

PREVENTATIVE MAINTENANCE

The bathroom sink needs a good flushing to clear buildup of hair and grease. Boil some water in a teapot and pour it down the sink. Boiled water is much hotter than tap water and will dissolve sludge coating the walls of your drainpipes. Do this once every two months or so and hopefully you'll avoid most clogs.

CAUTION

SLOWLY AND CAREFULLY

Use care while feeding the auger cable into the drain or horizontal pipe.

SELECTING AN AUGER

Drain augers are useful when a clog is too much to clear with plunging alone. The best auger is a coiled cable that wraps inside a housing. The housing should have a handle and a crank on it for spinning the cable inside the drain.

UNCLOGGING TOILETS

Do not continue to flush a clogged toilet. Flushing will not push objects through and will more likely flood the bathroom floor. Instead bail out the toilet until the bowl is about half full. The plunger needs some water to make a tight seal around the bowl. Most toilet clogs occur because the toilet trap is blocked. If a plunger or toilet auger fails to clear things up, the waste-vent stack may be blocked.

⚠ CAUTION

NO CHEMICALS ALLOWED

Never attempt to unclog a toilet with a chemical drain cleaner. Chances are it won't do the job, and you'll be forced to plunge or auger through a strong solution that could burn your skin or eyes.

HOW TO STOP A TOILET OVERFLOW

If the toilet begins to overflow, act fast. Remove everything on top of the tank and take off the lid. Pull the float up and push down on the flapper (at the tank bottom). The flush will stop.

1 PLUNGE THE TOILET WITH FORCE.

An ordinary plunger can clear a toilet, but the molded-cup type generates stronger suction. Work up and down vigorously for about a dozen strokes, then quickly yank away the plunger.

If the water disappears with a glug, it's likely the plunging has succeeded—but don't flush yet. Pour in more water and empty the bowl several times. If plunging doesn't work, you'll have to auger the toilet.

The auger's plastic cover protects the toilet

2 USE A CLOSET AUGER.

A closet auger makes short work of most toilet stoppages. This specialized tool has a long handle with a plastic cover at the bend to protect your toilet from scratches. To operate it, pull the spring all the way up into the handle (it will barely protrude from the plastic protective cover on the end of the auger). Insert the bit into the bowl outlet and crank. If you meet resistance, pull back slightly, wiggle the handle, and try again. A closet auger can grab and pull many blockages, but not solid objects such as toys. If you hear something other than the auger rattling around, remove the toilet to get at the item (see page 50).

Some objects defy ordinary removal techniques. Many of these clogs result when a small child places a toy in the toilet. No matter what you try, you can't pull the object back out. The answer may be to push or flush the object into a larger, downstream drainpipe. Then dislodge and remove the toy at a cleanout or trap. Just beware that pushing a blockage downstream may require hiring a plumber to remove the object, especially if there are no downstream traps or cleanouts.

Start with the highest cleanout you can find that is below the clogged fixture. If augering it does not work, continue working downward. An option is to go on the roof and run an auger through the vent stack. This job often warrants calling in a plumber or a drain-cleaning service, especially if the line is clogged with tree roots.

Practice preventative maintenance to avoid future clogs. Flush the drains once a week with hot tap water. This helps clear out residual soap, grease, and debris that enter the drainpipes with normal use. Clean drains once every six months using a noncaustic drain cleaner such as copper sulfide or sodium hydroxide. Noncaustic cleaners do not harm pipes; caustic cleaners do.

AUGER A CLEANOUT.

Look for a cleanout near the bottom of your home's soil stack. Loosen the plug of the cleanout. If water flows out, the blockage is below. (If no water flows out, the blockage may be holding the water above, so replace the cleanout plug and auger from a higher point.) Insert the auger and run it back and forth several times (see page 69).

USE A BLOW BAG.

Another solution is to use a blow bag. Hook the blow bag up to a garden hose and connect it to a hose bib or utility faucet. Thread the blow bag and the hose into the drain. Turn on the water supply. Be patient. It may take several minutes. Blow bags are most effective for clearing blockages in floor drains.

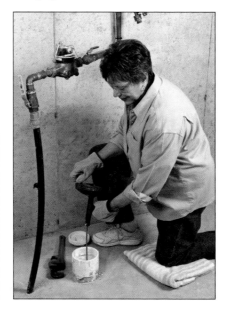

AUGER A HOUSE TRAP.

If neither procedure works, move farther down the line. Some houses have a house trap near the place where the drain line exits the house. Open one of the two plugs and thread in an auger. The blockage may be in the trap itself.

CAUTION

GET YOUR PAIL READY

Before removing a cleanout plug from a main drain line, grab some buckets to catch the wastewater.

1 REPLACE A CLEANOUT PLUG.

Be prepared for a mess. When removing a drain plug, you don't know what you'll find. Have rags and a bucket in place. Remove the cleanout plug with a pipe wrench. If you can't get the plug to move, give it a squirt or two of penetrating oil. Stubborn plugs may require brute force. Place a chisel on the edge of the plug and strike it with a hammer. If this doesn't work, you may have to break the plug.

2 INSTALL A PLASTIC PLUG . . .

The new plug will need a good seal. Paint the threads with pipe joint compound or wrap the threads with plumbers' tape.

OR INSTALL A RUBBER PLUG.

If the threads in the pipe are damaged, use an expandable rubber plug to seal the opening. Place the plug in the opening. Turn the wingnut until the rubber expands to seal the opening.

1 OPEN THE DRUM TRAP.

Many older bathrooms have a removable metal cap on the floor (usually near the tub), which covers a drum trap. Before opening it, bail out the tub and remove standing water with rags or a large sponge.

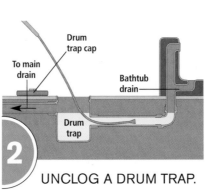

2 UNCLOG A DRUM TRAP.

Auger through the drum trap. You may have difficulty removing the cap. If a wrench doesn't do the trick, use a hammer and cold chisel or screwdriver. Damage the cap if necessary (you can replace it easily), but don't mar the threads on the trap. Open the trap slowly, watching for water to well up around the threads. If the trap is full, work the auger away from the tub toward the main drain. If the trap is only partially full (as shown), the obstruction is between the tub and the trap: Auger back and forth. Drum traps are no longer acceptable to code and must be replaced with a P-trap.

CLEAN A SEWER LINE.

If the blockage remains, the outdoor sewer line may be the problem. Often fine tree roots work their way into the line, creating an obstacle that only a heavy auger with a cutting bit can remove. First try using a garden hose to flush out the obstruction. If that doesn't work, call in a professional or rent a heavy-duty power auger. Running a power auger is a two-person job. Get a demonstration from the rental center.

If the water in your bathroom sink or tub gradually leaks out even though you've stopped the drain, or if it doesn't drain out as quickly as you'd like, you may need to adjust your drain assembly.

Before dismantling the assembly, pull up the strainer or stopper and remove any hair or other debris hanging from it. Thoroughly clean away soap or other gunk that may be keeping the strainer or stopper from seating properly.

YOU'LL NEED

TIME: An hour for most adjustments.

SKILLS: Basic plumbing skills.

TOOLS: Screwdriver, pliers.

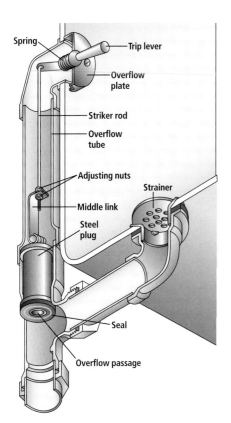

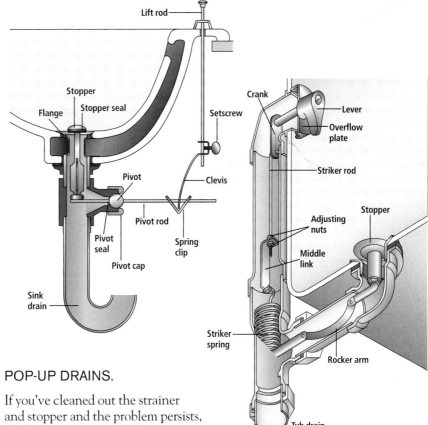

POP-UP DRAINS.

If you've cleaned out the strainer and stopper and the problem persists, check the stopper seal. If it's damaged, replace any rubber parts or replace the stopper itself. Look for signs of wear on the flange the stopper seats into.

On a bathroom sink, examine the pivot rod. When the stopper is closed, a working rod slants slightly up from the pivot to the clevis. If it doesn't, loosen the setscrew, raise or lower the clevis on the lift rod, and retighten the screw.

If the stopper doesn't operate as easily now as you would like, squeeze the spring clip, pull the pivot rod out

TRIP-LEVER DRAIN.

A trip lever lifts and lowers a seal plug at the base of the overflow tube. When the seal plug drops into its seat, water from the tub drain can't get past. But because the plug is hollow, water can still flow through the overflow tube.

of the clevis, and reinsert it into the next higher or lower hole. If water drips from the pivot, try tightening its cap. If the pivot still drips, you may need to replace the seal inside.

To adjust a tub pop-up, unscrew the overflow plate, withdraw the entire assembly, and loosen the adjusting nuts. If the stopper doesn't seat tightly, move the middle link higher on the striker rod. If the tub is slow to drain, lower the link.

Dismantle and adjust a trip lever as you would a tub pop-up unit. If the seal on the bottom of the plug appears worn, replace it.

If your showerhead sprays unevenly, take it apart and clean it or replace it. If it leaks at the arm, or if it doesn't stay in position, tighten the retainer or collar nut. If that doesn't work, replace the O-ring—or replace the showerhead.

If you want to replace your showerhead, take the old one with you to your supplier to make sure you get one that will fit the arm or pipe. You'll find a wide range of styles and features.

YOU'LL NEED

TIME: About an hour for removal and scrubbing; overnight soaking for a thorough cleaning.

SKILLS: Basic plumbing skills.

TOOLS: Wrench, screwdriver, pointed tool or thin wire, toothbrush.

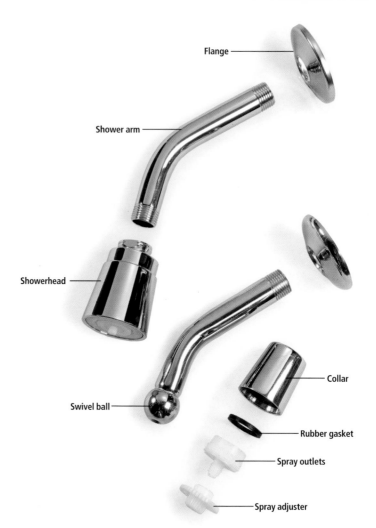

Flange — Shower arm — Showerhead — Swivel ball — Collar — Rubber gasket — Spray outlets — Spray adjuster

Shower arm — Nut

REMOVING A SHOWERHEAD.

This is a simple matter of unscrewing the nut at the shower arm. Take care not to mar the finish of the showerhead or arm: Use a wrench rather than pliers, and as an added precaution, cushion your tool with a rag as you work.

TWO BASIC TYPES.

Newer showerheads screw onto the shower arm, the chrome pipe that extends from the wall. Older models require a shower arm with a ball-shape end that acts as a swivel. In most cases, you can switch to a newer style if you replace the shower arm. To do so, remove the shower arm from its connection. Wrap plumber's tape around the threads of the new shower arm before screwing it into place.

CLEAN THE HOLES

Showerheads spray unevenly when the tiny holes have gotten clogged with mineral deposits. Use an old toothbrush to clean the head. Then run a sharp blast of water backward through the showerhead.

DISMANTLE AND CLEAN

For a thorough cleaning, take the head apart, use a pin to poke out any mineral buildup or debris, and brush away all deposits. Then soak the parts in vinegar overnight to dissolve remaining mineral deposits. Reassemble and reinstall.

A slight leak under the sink at the tailpiece is likely the result of a poor seal between the strainer body and the sink.

To check for this, plug the sink, fill the bowl, and look for drips.

If water drips from the place where the strainer body joins the sink, disassemble the strainer and apply new putty. Leaks also may occur where the tailpiece joins the strainer body. If so, tighten the slip nut. If that does not solve the problem, replace the washer.

YOU'LL NEED

TIME: About two hours to disassemble and reassemble a strainer.

SKILLS: Intermediate plumbing skills.

TOOLS: Adjustable wrench (and possibly a spud wrench), putty knife, plumber's putty, joint compound. You may need replacement parts.

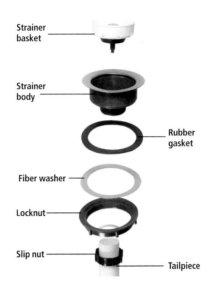

Strainer basket

Strainer body

Rubber gasket

Fiber washer

Locknut

Slip nut

Tailpiece

SINK STRAINER PARTS.

The sink strainer captures waste that otherwise would clog the drain. Its wide bowl is held snug against the sink bottom by the locknut. Putty and a rubber gasket sandwich the sink for a tight seal. The strainer body connects to the tailpiece with a washer and a slip nut.

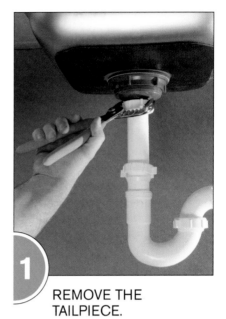

1 REMOVE THE TAILPIECE.

Use an adjustable wrench to loosen the slip nut beneath the strainer body and the slip nut above the trap bend. Finish unscrewing it by hand, then remove the tailpiece.

Locknut

2 REMOVE THE LOCKNUT.

You may have difficulty removing the locknut, especially if it is hard to get at. Consider purchasing a spud wrench, which is specially designed to fit on locknuts. Or tap gently with a hammer and screwdriver to loosen the nut.

3 REMOVE OLD PUTTY.

Use a putty knife to scrape the old putty from the drain opening. Clean the opening thoroughly with a scouring pad soaked with paint thinner. If you plan to reuse the strainer, clean off the flange of the strainer as well.

4 APPLY PUTTY AND REINSTALL.

Make a rope of putty and place it on the lip of the drain opening. Press the strainer into the opening. From under the sink, slip on the rubber gasket and the friction ring; screw on the locknut. Tighten the locknut until the strainer nests completely into the sink. Reinstall the tailpiece.

INSTALLING A WATER HAMMER ARRESTOR

If you hear what sounds like banging pipes when your clothes washer (or other appliance) is at work, the noise is referred to as water hammer. Water hammer occurs when water moves through a pipe and the outlet valve is closed. The pressure created can reach 60 times that of the water moving through the pipe—upwards of 600 pounds per square inch on the system. Over time, water hammer results in the failure of fittings. Many local codes require installers to put water hammer arrestors on appliances that have quick-closing valves.

YOU'LL NEED

TIME: About two hours.

SKILLS: Soldering copper pipe, connecting fittings.

TOOLS: Measuring tape, pipe wrenches, tubing cutter, propane torch, reaming tool, wire brush, flux brush, flux, spark lighter, solder.

1 TURN OFF WATER.

Turn off the water supply at a downstream valve. Open a faucet at a lower elevation to drain the water in the system. Mark the location for the arrestor on the existing pipe. Leave enough pipe so each side will seat firmly in the new fitting.

2 CUT THE PIPE.

Use a tubing cutter or hacksaw to cut the copper pipe. Make sure the cut is straight. Copper pipe must be completely dry before soldering. Place bits of white bread in the pipe to remove remaining water near the opening. The bread soaks up the water, eventually disintegrates, and flushes through the system.

3 CONNECT THE TEE.

Smooth the edges of the copper pipe using a reamer, emery cloth, and wire brush. Apply flux to all connecting surfaces. Assemble the connection. Make sure the end of each pipe seats firmly in each fitting. Solder the tee to the pipe. Heat the pipe evenly with a propane torch, then apply solder in a continuous bead (see pages 142–145).

4 ATTACH NIPPLE AND ADAPTER.

In tight places, place a metal sheet behind the pipe to protect subflooring and flammable objects. Solder a copper nipple to the tee. Connect the reducing female adapter.

5 INSTALL THE HAMMER ARRESTOR.

Install the threaded water hammer arrestor and tighten by hand. Use two pipe wrenches to tighten one-quarter turn.

MAINTAINING A CLOTHES WASHER

Clothes washers are designed to be durable and last 10 to 15 years. Keeping them in good working condition requires periodic maintenance. Most washer surfaces are coated with a porcelain enamel, which is very resistant to staining. However, long-term exposure to chemicals can damage the appliance's surfaces. Promptly wipe up any spills with a damp cloth or paper towel.

As a rule, replace inlet hoses every five years. Periodically inspect and replace the hoses if bulges, kinks, cuts, wear, or leaks are discovered.

If you will not be using your washer for an extended period of time, give it a true break. Unplug the washer, and turn off the water supply (reducing the likelihood that a hose will burst and flood your house while you are away). Leave the door open to provide ventilation.

Depending on the hardness of your water supply, plan on cleaning or replacing the washer's inlet screens. Sediment builds up over time, clogging the flow of water to the machine.

1 DISCONNECT THE HOSES.

Unplug the washer and move it away from the wall so you can access the hose connections at the back of the washer. Turn off the valves that control hot and cold water flowing to the hoses. Use pliers to unscrew and disconnect the hoses. Drain water in the hoses into a bucket or the floor drain.

2 REMOVE THE SCREENS.

Use tweezers or needle-nose pliers to pry out the inlet screens. Inlet screens prevent debris from entering the washer. If you rip or crinkle a screen, or if you don't want to bother with cleaning, replace both screens. They are available at hardware stores and home centers.

YOU'LL NEED

TIME: Approximately one hour, plus time for screens to soak overnight.

SKILLS: Soldering copper pipe, connecting fittings.

TOOLS: Measuring tape, pipe wrenches, tubing cutter, propane torch, reaming tool, wire brush, flux brush, flux, spark lighter, solder.

3 CLEAN AND REPLACE THE SCREENS.

If the screens are crusted with mineral deposits, soak them overnight in white vinegar or a cleaning product made for

loosening hard water buildup. Use an old toothbrush to clean any remaining deposits. Rinse with running water until the screen is completely clean.

Use a tweezers or needle-nose pliers to carefully reposition the inlet screens in the washer.

Attach the hot and cold water lines to the inlet openings. Screw the hoses back on, then tighten with groove-joint pliers. Turn the water back on and check for leaks; you may need to tighten the hose connections further. Push the washer back in place and check to make sure it is level. Add shims or adjust the feet under the washer until it's level.

REPLACING A SUMP PUMP

A sump pump assists in removing water from a wet basement, transforming it into usable space. But before you run out and buy a sump pump, first identify the source of water in the basement. If water seeps into your basement because of a high water table, removing the water with a sump pump is the answer.

When water enters the basement through leaking foundation walls, explore options to seal the basement and transport the outside water away from the foundation. Also check the external perimeter around the foundation. There should be a mound of soil that slopes away from the foundation, carrying surface water into the yard. If not, build up the soil level. It will help direct water away from the basement.

A ⅓-horsepower sump pump will meet the needs of most homes. Consider a ½-horsepower pump if a ⅓-horsepower pump will not keep up with the water. Getting an exact answer as to which size is needed is determined by the area of drainage connected to the sump, the depth to groundwater, the basement depth, and other factors. Rather than going through a jumble of calculations, talk to your home center or hardware retailer about which pump is best for your situation.

If replacing a sump pump, you most likely will not be running new discharge pipe.

YOU'LL NEED

TIME: Half a day to a full day.

SKILLS: Working with and connecting plastic fittings, drilling.

TOOLS: Keyhole saw, power drill, caulking gun, screwdriver, level.

PVC VS. ABS

When installing discharge pipe, some codes allow you to use either PVC or ABS. One disadvantage with ABS is that it tends to become brittle over time and then is susceptible to cracking. Check your local codes before using ABS.

CAUTION

DON'T DISCHARGE INTO THE SEPTIC SYSTEM

Never discharge a sump pump into a septic system, sewer drain, or floor drain. During wet conditions the septic system drainage field is typically saturated trying to handle the normal flow of wastewater. The discharge from a sump pump can damage the septic system and kill the bacteria necessary to digest the waste.

REMOVE THE OLD SUMP PUMP.

Unplug the power cord for the sump pump. If the cord is taped to the discharge pipe, remove the tape, freeing the cord. There should be a rubber coupling with clamps that connects the sump pump to a check valve and to the discharge line. Disconnect the clamps and remove the rubber coupling. Inspect the coupling for damage and replace it, if necessary. Lift the old sump pump out of the pit.

ASSEMBLE THE SUMP PUMP.

Determine the placement of the new sump pump and measure the lengths needed for the discharge piping. The sump pump and the discharge fitting are not normally preassembled, so you will need to put them together. Follow the manufacturer's assembly instructions.

3 SET PUMP IN THE PIT.

Position the pump so the float is a couple of inches below the floor surface. The sump pump requires a solid base that will withstand water and prevent the pump from moving. Tamp the gravel. If the base is still not solid, stabilize the pump with a small brick or piece of concrete. Do not use wood.

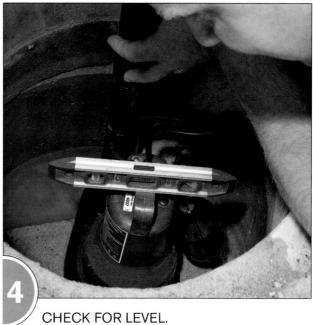

4 CHECK FOR LEVEL.

Use a small torpedo level to make sure the pump housing is level and that the discharge pipe is plumb. If necessary, adjust the discharge pipe and shim the housing with plastic shims. Do not use wood shims.

AVOID AN ENDLESS CYCLE

When installing a discharge pipe through the foundation, add enough length to carry the water away from the foundation. Dumping too close to the foundation may result in the water finding its way back into the sump pit. This just creates an endless cycle. Ideally, water should be discharged at least 20 feet from the house. This is not always possible in a residential area. Use common sense. Be careful not to discharge onto a neighbor's lot or septic drainage field.

5 CONNECT THE DISCHARGE LINE.

Position a rubber coupling on the check valve. Place two hose clamps over the rubber coupling. Slide one clamp over the check valve and tighten. Slide the other clamp over the sump pump discharge pipe and tighten it. If you don't have a check valve on the discharge line, install one to prevent water from backing up into the sump pump. Run the power cord along the discharge pipe, fastening it to the pipe with electrician's tape. Adjust the float to the level recommended by the manufacturer. Plug the pump cord into a nearby GFCI-protected receptacle. Pour a 5-gallon bucket of water into the sump pit to test it.

Major
IMPROVEMENTS AND REPAIRS

One morning while you're standing outside your bathroom waiting for your son or daughter to finish getting ready for school, you dream of adding that second or third bathroom. How nice it would be to have your own space! Maybe you could add a shower, or better yet, a whirlpool bath in a new master suite. Now *that* would be the life. You wonder if you have enough money to hire a plumber to build your dream, and that's when the dream ends. Plumbers are expensive.

But you can still live your dream. The answer lies in the following projects, which explain the step-by-step process for plumbing your haven. Learn how to plan for new fixtures, build a control riser for a shower and tub installation, install a sink and toilet, and yes, how to install a whirlpool bath. Soon enough you'll be soaking in that tub, wondering why you waited so long to do it yourself.

UPGRADE FOR CONVENIENCE AND STYLE.

Innovative design layout with an eye on functionality adds up to a hardworking kitchen installation. The rimmed sink (pages 99–100) in the corner frees up countertop surface area. A single-handle faucet accents the fun simplicity of the decor, while the water dispenser (pages 125–126) efficiently provides a hot cup of water. A dishwasher (pages 123–124) near the sink allows for easy cleanup.

INSTALL RELAXATION.

This tub, with its simple curved form, caresses away the edges of the workday. Lightweight construction facilitates installation. The fixtures are easy to reach both within or from outside the tub.

PLUMBED FOR FLEXIBILITY.

A clever use of the standard three-hole sink allows for installation of a single-handle faucet, an air gap for the dishwasher, an under-sink filtered drinking faucet, and a hot water dispenser. The faucet's pullout spout is handy for cleaning or rinsing vegetables in either sink.

Most improvements shown in this book are add-ons, those that connect new fittings or fixtures to existing pipes. Running new lines requires an understanding of how supply, drain, and vent pipes work in general and of your home's system in particular.

New supply lines are the easiest to plan. They require no slope or venting, just the correct pipe size (see box). You can run them almost anywhere you need them.

Far trickier are the drain-waste-vent (DWV) lines that carry away water, waste, and gases. The illustration right and on page 88 show straightforward ways to tap in to accommodate a new fixture. Your situation may be more complex and may require the skill of a professional.

For a new installation, even a minor one, you'll need to apply to your local building department for a permit. Be sure to arrange to have the work inspected *before* you cover up new pipes.

SIZING SUPPLY LINES

Check with your local building department for the size of the supply line required. As a general rule, most departments require that a line supplying one or two fixtures be ½ inch. Lines that supply three or more fixtures must be at least ¾ inch.

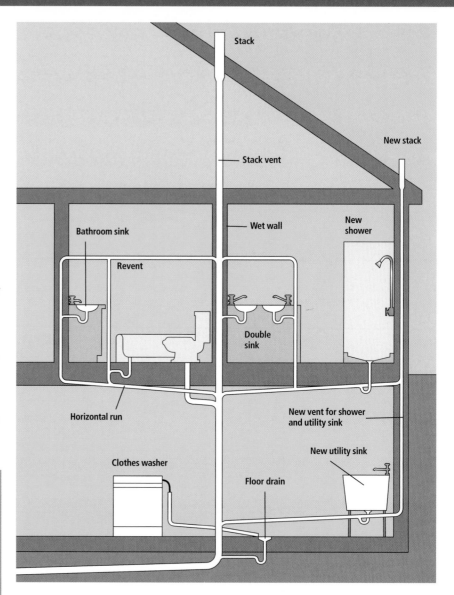

Stack

Stack vent

New stack

Bathroom sink

Wet wall

New shower

Revent

Double sink

Horizontal run

New vent for shower and utility sink

New utility sink

Clothes washer

Floor drain

PLANNING DRAIN LINES.

The first step in planning an extension to your plumbing system is to map out exactly where existing lines run. Your home probably has a drainage arrangement similar to the one shown. Notice that some of the fixtures (toilet, double sink) cluster near a wet wall, which contains the main stack. A wet wall is usually a few inches thicker than other walls to accommodate the 3- or 4-inch-diameter stack that runs up through the roof. (One way to find a wet wall is to note the location of the stack on the roof.)

The fixtures drain directly into the main stack or into horizontal runs that slope downward at a pitch of at least ¼ inch per running foot. Fixtures more than a few feet from the stack (such as the bathtub and bathroom sink) must be vented with a loop that goes up and back to the stack. Called a revent or circuit vent, this branch is concealed inside walls and floors of normal thickness. Fixtures even farther away (such as the shower and utility sink) may require a separate stack. Requirements vary on revents and new vents, so check local codes.

Position the new fixtures as close as possible to an existing stack to minimize necessary wall damage.

FORM AND FUNCTION

A beautifully designed fixture that is not practical for the way you use the kitchen will eventually frustrate you to the point of replacing it. For example, a dishwasher that's not conveniently located near a sink necessitates additional trips back and forth—as well as additional plumbing. If you need a sink in two locations, consider installing two.

STORAGE OPPORTUNITY

Long vanities that house double sinks are convenient, but they consume a lot of space. Installing a center vanity flanked with pedestal sinks provides necessary storage for accessories while foregoing the feel of a large enclosed area. These bookend pedestal sinks lend balance and symmetry.

GUEST-SUITE DINING

Even a small amount of space was enough to transform this guest room into a guest suite. The rimmed sink (pages 99–100), faucet (pages 42–45), and sprayer are features your guests will appreciate.

VENTING POSSIBILITIES

Think of a main stack as a two-way chimney: Water and wastes go down; gases go up. Just as you wouldn't install a fireplace without a chimney, neither should you consider adding a fixture without properly venting it. Strangle the air supply of a drain, and you risk creating a siphoning effect that sucks water out of traps. This, in turn, breaks the seal that provides protection from gas backup—and often retards the flow of wastes as well.

Codes specifically state how you must vent fixtures. These requirements differ from one locality to another, so check your community's regulations for details about the systems shown here.

With unit venting—sometimes referred to as common venting—two similar fixtures share the same stack fitting. This method allows you to put a new fixture back-to-back with one that already exists. The fixtures are installed on opposite sides of the wet wall. To install a unit vent, open up the wall, replace the existing sanitary tee with a sanitary cross, and connect both traps to it. The drains of unit-vented fixtures must be set at equal heights.

Wet venting uses a section of one fixture's drain line to double as the vent for another. Some codes forbid wet venting. Those that allow it often specify that the vertical drain must be at least one pipe size larger than the upper fixture drain. In no case can the vertical drain be smaller than the lower drain.

Regardless of how you vent a fixture, codes limit the distance between the trap outlet and the vent.

These distances depend on the size of the drain line you're running. For 1¼-, 1½-, and 2-inch drain lines—the sizes you'll most likely be working with—2, 3, and 5 feet, respectively, are typical distances. (If you're adding plastic drain line, see page 94. For how to tap into a cast-iron drain, see page 95.)

Often the best way to install a new fixture is with a revent, or circuit vent, but clear this with your local building department before you decide to do it. Some codes forbid you to use this solution with heavy-use items such as toilets or showers.

Sometimes the only solution is to install a separate vent that runs through the roof (see pages 96–97). If the fixture will be installed on the top floor, it'll be relatively simple.

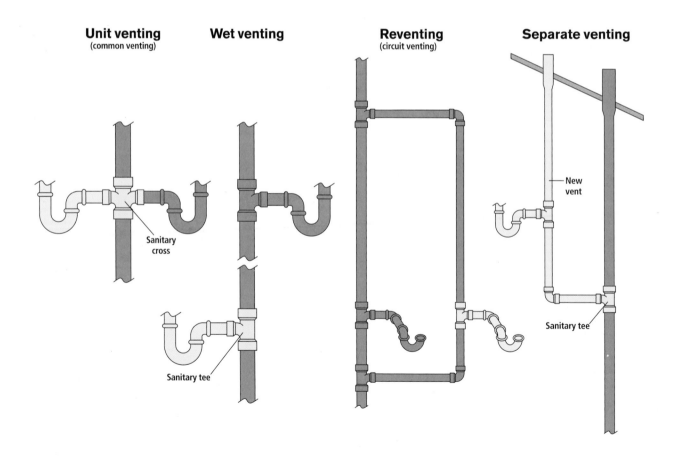

Unit venting
(common venting)

Wet venting

Reventing
(circuit venting)

Separate venting

Sanitary cross

Sanitary tee

New vent

Sanitary tee

ROUGHING-IN TUBS, SHOWERS, AND TOILETS

Plan the location of your bathroom fixtures carefully: A few inches one way or the other make the difference between a bathroom that is comfortable and one that feels cramped and inconvenient.

First map the floor of your bathroom on a piece of graph paper. Then cut out small-scale pieces of paper to represent the fixtures. Move the pieces until you find the most usable configuration. If a door opens inward, make sure it swings completely without hitting a fixture.

The dimensions given in the drawings at right show the minimum requirements for ease of use. Do not place fixtures closer to each other than specified. Once you decide on your floor plan, mark your floors and walls for the rough-in dimensions, using the dimensions shown below.

Once you decide on a layout that will fit your needs, use masking tape or a carpenter's pencil to mark the locations of fixtures and pipes on the walls and floor. If you are remodeling a room that you don't want to mark or tape, use tacky-back notes to mark the walls—the newer super-self-sticking notes are ideal, won't fall off the wall over time, and won't damage wallpaper or paint. It also helps to place the fixtures on the floor and outline them. Take care to consider the placement of cabinets when laying out the water supply and drain cleanouts. You may want to temporarily position the cabinets where they will be installed before you complete the supply and drainpipe layouts. When you have completed the layout, measure and adjust the arrangement until all fixtures meet the minimum clearance specifications of the manufacturer and you are comfortable with the layout.

Placing the fixtures (minimum allowances)

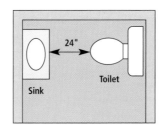

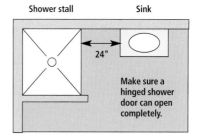

Make sure a hinged shower door can open completely.

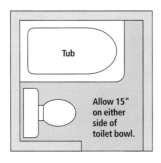

Allow 15" on either side of toilet bowl.

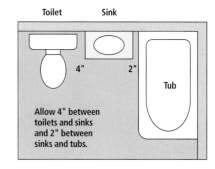

Allow 4" between toilets and sinks and 2" between sinks and tubs.

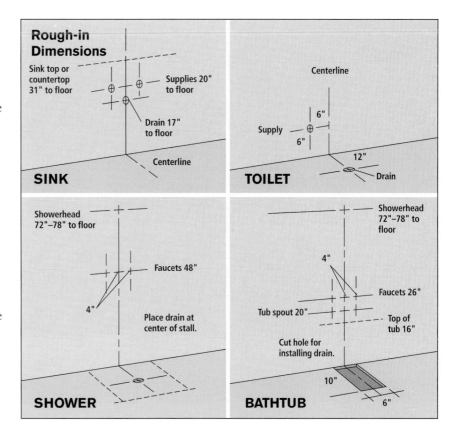

Rough-in Dimensions

SINK
- Sink top or countertop 31" to floor
- Supplies 20" to floor
- Drain 17" to floor
- Centerline

TOILET
- Centerline
- Supply
- 6"
- 6"
- 12"
- Drain

SHOWER
- Showerhead 72"–78" to floor
- Faucets 48"
- 4"
- Place drain at center of stall.

BATHTUB
- Showerhead 72"–78" to floor
- 4"
- Faucets 26"
- Tub spout 20"
- Top of tub 16"
- Cut hole for installing drain.
- 10"
- 6"

Roughing in tub, shower, and toilets *(continued)*

Once your plans are ready, cut holes in your walls and floors for installing drain lines and supply stubs—the supply lines that stick out a bit from the wall and are ready to accept stop valves.

Patching walls and floors can be more time-consuming than the plumbing itself. Where possible, limit your cuts to areas that the fixtures will cover. Cut drywall or plaster neatly so you can patch it easily. Don't forget to install venting (see pages 86–88).

FINDING DRAINPIPES

In order to rough in your new drains, you need to know where the existing drain is. Start in the basement or crawlspace. If you see a 3- or 4-inch stack, it probably runs straight through the roof. If not, look for a plumbing access panel. You may find it on the wall opposite your bathroom fixtures. (Often it's in a closet.) Remove the access panel and peer inside with a flashlight.

If you notice a wall is thicker than the standard 4½ inches, it probably contains drainpipes. Toilets usually are placed near stacks.

YOU'LL NEED

TIME: Roughly two days to cut walls and rough-in a sink, toilet, and tub or shower.

SKILLS: Basic plumbing and carpentry skills.

TOOLS: Reciprocating saw, basic plumbing tools, basic carpentry tools.

Supply stub   Trap adapter   Supply stub

1½" or 1¼" drainpipe

ROUGH-IN A SINK.

If you are installing a vanity cabinet, you have latitude for placing the drain and supply stubs. For a wall-hung sink or a pedestal sink, hold the fixture up against the wall and mark the best locations for drain and supply stubs (see pages 99–103). In most cases, it is best to position the supply stubs within 12 inches of the faucet.

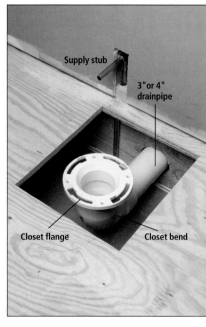

Supply stub

3" or 4" drainpipe

Closet flange   Closet bend

ROUGH-IN A TOILET.

Be careful to place the closet bend the correct distance from the wall—usually 12 inches to the center of the drain. (Double-check the requirements for your toilet.) You'll place a closet flange on top of the floor after you have patched and surfaced it. Only a cold water supply stub is needed. Place it 6 inches above the floor and to the left of the drainpipe.

STAY GROUNDED

Install a jumper wire and ground clamps when you install plastic pipe that separates a section of metal pipe. Many homes use metal plumbing in the electrical grounding system. Jumper wires keep the grounding system intact and keep your home safe.

DRAINAGE DYNAMICS

Plan new drainpipe in walls so they slope toward the branch or main drain stack. A fall of ¼ inch for every foot is best.

When a fixture is greater than 3 feet away from a stack, connect it to a vent pipe that joins a stack or exits through the roof. Check your local building codes for requirements.

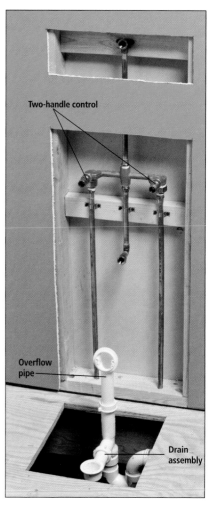

ROUGH-IN A SHOWER.

To correctly position the drain, set the base in place and measure from the walls. Allow for wall surfacing (see pages 104–110). To spare patching later, cut the floor so the base will cover the hole. Install a P-trap below the level of the floor, at the level the drain assembly kit requires. Install the control assembly. Its size determines how far apart the supply pipes must be. Firmly attach the shower pipe to framing.

ROUGH-IN A TUB AND SHOWER.

Cut the floor so the tub will cover the hole. Install a P-trap and bathtub drain assembly. It will be somewhat unstable until you connect it to the tub. The one-handle control shown requires that you plumb the supply lines horizontally into it. Attach the control and the top of the shower pipe firmly to framing; you will probably need to frame in a piece of lumber between the studs.

ROUGH-IN A TWO-HANDLE CONTROL.

A two-handle control is easier to install. Set the hot and cold pipes at the same height. Attach the control and the top of the shower pipe elbow to frame supports.

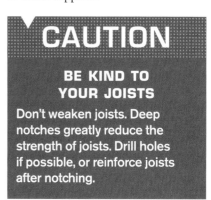

CAUTION

BE KIND TO YOUR JOISTS

Don't weaken joists. Deep notches greatly reduce the strength of joists. Drill holes if possible, or reinforce joists after notching.

TAPPING INTO EXISTING LINES

When you add a sink close to or on the other side of a wet wall—the wall that contains working plumbing lines—you can tie into existing copper supplies and plastic drain lines. (For tapping into cast-iron, see page 95.) If you have trouble locating the drain line, see the tips on page 90.

Tapping into a wet wall is much easier than installing new drain, vent, and supply lines, but it is still a major project. Don't spoil the job by getting an important detail wrong: A telltale sign of an unprofessional plumbing job is revealed when the hot and cold faucets end up on the wrong sides of the sink. Be sure the hot handle is on the left.

YOU'LL NEED

TIME: About a day.

SKILLS: Joining copper or plastic pipe, basic carpentry skills.

TOOLS: Keyhole saw, utility knife, tubing cutter, fine-tooth saw, miter box, groove-joint pliers, hacksaw or reciprocating saw, ratchet with socket, torch.

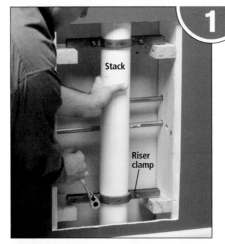

1 **ANCHOR THE DRAIN LINE.**

Shut off the water and drain the lines. Open up the wet wall to the center of the studs on either side, so you will have a nailing surface for patching later. You may have to make a separate hole for access to the supply pipes. To anchor the stack, attach riser clamps above and below the area you will cut.

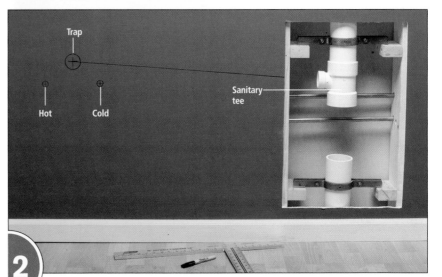

2 **LAY OUT THE INSTALLATION.**

Plan out the fixture's rough-in dimensions (see pages 89–91) and mark them on the wall. Be sure the location doesn't exceed the maximum distance local codes permit. To determine the point at which the fixture will tie into the stack, draw a line that slopes from the center of the drain trap at ¼ inch per foot. Being careful to cut squarely, use a hacksaw or reciprocating saw to remove a section of stack 8 inches longer than the sanitary tee you'll install.

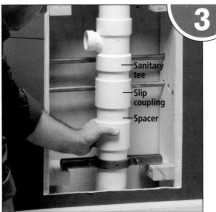

3 **INSTALL THE SANITARY TEE.**

In most cases, you'll need a sanitary tee to accept 1½-inch pipe; for bathroom sinks, 1¼-inch is sometimes acceptable. Dry-fit the tee, two spacers, and two slip couplings into place as shown. Don't cement them until the rest of the run is completed. Slide the couplings up and down to secure the spacers.

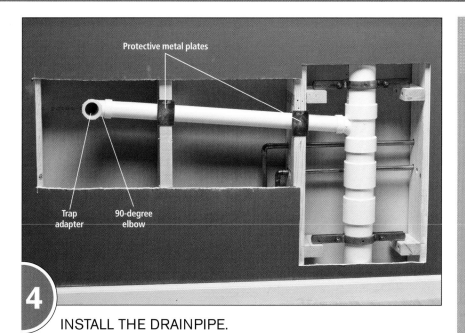

Protective metal plates

Trap adapter

90-degree elbow

4 INSTALL THE DRAINPIPE.

Cut out a strip of drywall and notch the studs just deep enough to support the pipes. Use a 45-degree elbow and a short spacer at the stack, and a 90-degree elbow and a trap adapter at the trap. Once you're sure the pipe slopes at ¼ inch per foot, scribe all the pieces with alignment marks, then disassemble, prime, and cement the drainpipe pieces together (see pages 151–155).

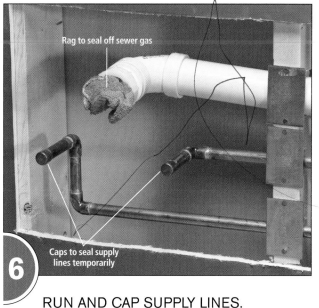

Rag to seal off sewer gas

Caps to seal supply lines temporarily

5 INSTALL SUPPLY TEES.

Tap into copper or plastic supply lines using spacers, slip couplings, and tees similar to those used on the drainpipe. (For soldering copper joints, see pages 142–145.) If you tap into galvanized steel supply lines, you may have to cut and remove sections of pipe and install union connectors. Be sure to use a transition fitting if you're mixing pipe materials, such as copper and iron (see pages 134–135).

6 RUN AND CAP SUPPLY LINES.

Run pipes to the fixture location using 90-degree elbows and pipe as needed. Use 90-degree elbows and short pieces to bring the lines out past the wall surface. Stuff a rag in the drain to seal off sewer gas. Solder caps on the ends of the supply lines, turn on the water, and test for leaks. Close up the wall, add stop valves (see page 26), and you're ready to install the fixture.

ADDING PLASTIC DRAIN LINES

Cutting, moving, and refitting plastic pipe are all simple jobs—as long as you have a plastic waste stack and easy access to the drainpipe.

Every drain line must be properly vented (see pages 86–88). Be sure you have this planned before you cut into the drainpipe. You may need to tap in at a second, higher point for the vent.

1 CUT OUT A SECTION OF PIPE.

Measure the new sanitary tee to see how much of the old pipe you need to remove. Take into account the depth of the sockets (see pages 136–137). Be sure that both sides of the existing pipe are supported, so they'll stay in position after the cut is made. Cut with a hacksaw or fine-tooth saw and remove any burrs with a utility knife.

2 DRY-FIT THE SANITARY TEE.

Install the top end first, then the bottom. You may have to loosen one of your support straps somewhere to give yourself enough play in the pipes to do this. Once the sanitary tee is in the desired position, make an alignment mark with a marker.

3 CUT HOLE AND INSTALL NEW PIPE.

Run pipes to the location of the new fixture (see pages 89–91). If you need to run the drainpipe through wall plates or framing, cut holes to accommodate the pipe. Leave at least ⅝ inch of wood on any side that will receive drywall. This way, nails or screws driven through drywall and into the plate won't pierce the pipe.

4 CONNECT THE PIECES.

Connect the new drainpipe to the sanitary tee with elbows and lengths of pipe. Dry-fit the pieces, draw alignment lines, disassemble, prime, and cement the pieces together (see pages 152–155). Support the run with at least one strap for the horizontal run.

CAUTION

PROTECT YOUR EYES

This is a job in which plenty of dirt, burrs, and sawdust will fall from above. Wear goggles when working above your head.

TAPPING INTO CAST-IRON DRAIN LINES

Cast-iron pipe was commonly used for the drain-waste-vent system in older homes. Often one or two large stacks are made of cast-iron and the lines leading into them are galvanized steel.

Cast-iron is difficult to work with (see Caution below) and, fortunately, it is no longer required for new installations. However, you may need to run a new drain into an existing cast-iron stack. Most likely, you will have to tap in at two places: one for the drain and one for the vent.

This page shows how to break into a cast-iron stack to replace a cast-iron Y-fitting with a plastic sanitary tee. You'll use the same techniques to install a sanitary tee, as shown on page 94.

as shown on page 94.

CAUTION

CONSIDER HIRING A PRO

Working with cast-iron is difficult and can be dangerous. Cast-iron is heavy, is prone to shattering, and has sharp edges. This is a project that you may want to leave to a professional. Some plumbers will make the cast-iron connections only, allowing you to save money by making the plastic connections yourself.

YOU'LL NEED

TIME: Set aside a full day, so you can take your time on this difficult project.

SKILLS: Joining plastic pipe and basic carpentry skills.

TOOLS: Cast-iron pipe cutter (rent this tool), socket and ratchet, screwdriver, hacksaw or fine-tooth saw.

1 SUPPORT THE STACK.

Securely support the stack from above and make sure it is well-supported below. (You do not need to move either portion of the cast-iron pipe in order to make the connection.) Use riser clamps specially made for support.

2 CUT THE PIPE.

Rent a chain-type pipe cutter. Wrap the chain around the stack and hook it. Then, with the handles open, crank the chain tight with the turn screw. Draw the handles together. This part of the job takes muscle, but if you follow the tool manufacturer's directions, you will get a clean cut.

3 FINISH CUTTING, REMOVE FITTING.

If you are removing a fitting, make a second cut about 4 inches below the first cut, and cut the horizontal run. If the horizontal pipe is galvanized steel, cut it with a hacksaw. Remove the 4-inch section and pull out the fitting.

4 INSTALL NO-HUB FITTINGS.

Install new plastic fittings with no-hub connectors. You may have to use short sections of pipe as spacers. To assemble a no-hub connector, slip the connector over the end of the old pipe, insert the sanitary tee with spacers in place, slide the connector so it bridges the old pipe and the spacers, and install clamps. Tighten clamps with a screwdriver.

ADDING NEW VENTS

If your new fixture is located far from an existing stack, codes may require a new vent. Though you'll have to run the new vent all the way through the roof, doing so may be easier than tying into the existing stack. You'll create less work adding a new stack than you would by reventing and patching, especially if your wall is void of insulation and fire blocking. If you have attic space with exposed pipes, consider running the new vent straight up through the attic. You can tie into the existing vent there. Unlike drainpipes, vent pipes can run horizontally since gases are drawn upward through the vent by the lower atmospheric pressure outside the house.

Calculating drain and vent size for shared fixtures can be daunting. Each fixture added to the system has a unit rating, which is a measure of the peak flow of discharge through a drainpipe. For example, a unit rating of a typical bathroom sink is 7½ gallons per minute. To accurately determine the vent size, you will need to add together the ratings of each fixture that shares a common drain or vent. Fortunately you can save yourself the time of calculating vent size, because the typical bathroom with a toilet, sink, and combination shower and bathtub can be adequately served with a 2-inch vent. Local codes vary, so check with your building inspector for vent size. If you're not installing a toilet, a bathroom sink and bathtub can share a 1½-inch vent.

YOU'LL NEED

TIME: If there are no major obstructions, count on spending a day running the vent and a day patching the walls.

SKILLS: Basic plumbing and carpentry skills.

TOOLS: Drill with holesaw bit, knife, keyhole saw, jigsaw.

Holesaw bit

1 CUT HOLE FOR VENT PIPE.

In the attic, find the top plate of the wall where the new vent is needed. Choose a spot between two studs and drill through the plate. Size the hole so it's just big enough to handle the outside diameter of the pipe. (Check local codes; they usually call for a 1½- or 1¼-inch vent.)

2 INSTALL ROOF VENT.

Mark the point directly above the hole and drive a nail up through the roof. Remove a shingle; cut a hole with a jigsaw or reciprocating saw. (You may need to cut a larger hole if you're increasing pipe size. See Step 4.) If a rafter is in the way, offset the vent with 45-degree elbows.

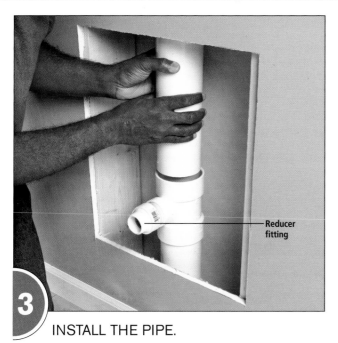

3 INSTALL THE PIPE.

Reducer fitting

With a helper, slide a pipe through the holes. Start at the attic and push down. After everything is dry-fit, prime and cement the joints. Allow for about two feet of pipe to extend above the roof—you can trim it as soon as the cement has set and you have checked the fit of the flashing.

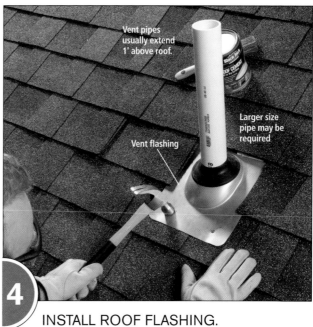

Vent pipes usually extend 1' above roof.

Larger size pipe may be required

Vent flashing

4 INSTALL ROOF FLASHING.

Secure the vent with a riser clamp (see page 92) in the attic. In cold climates, codes call for an increased pipe size where the pipe pierces the roof. This prevents freeze-ups from clogging the vent. Slip the flashing over the vent; tuck it under the shingles uphill from the vent. Seal with roofing cement.

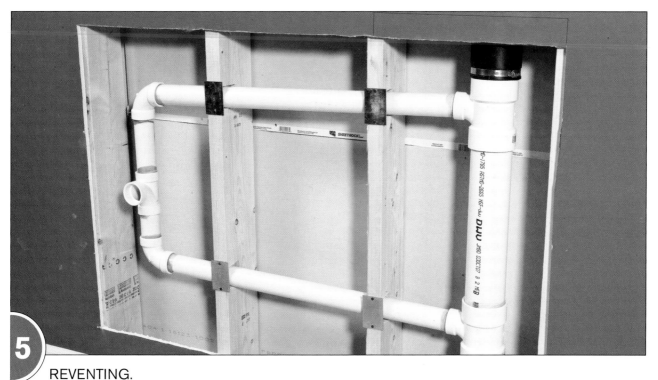

5 REVENTING.

If your new appliance is close enough to an existing stack, it is often easiest to revent. However, as the photo shows, this usually means a major patching job afterward. If you will be tying into an old cast-iron stack, you will have to go through the steps on page 95.

RUNNING THE SUPPLY LINES

Once the DWV system is installed, you must tackle the easier job of extending supply lines to the new location. If you are tying into old galvanized pipe, look for a convenient union fitting, open it, and dismantle back to the nearest fittings. Otherwise, tee in the supply by cutting a supply pipe and removing both ends (see page 92). Now you are ready to connect new to old. Turn the water off and drain the lines before cutting pipe or opening unions.

MAINTAINING PRESSURE WHEN ADDING LINES

For pipes that supply more than two fixtures, use ¾-inch rather than ½-inch pipe.

If you have a long run (more than 25 feet), use ¾-inch pipe. Usually it is best to run ¾-inch pipe into a bathroom, then ½-inch pipe to each fixture.

Don't move up from ½-inch to ¾-inch pipe in a line. Step down in dimension, never up.

If you have more than four right-angle bends, make some of them gradual using 45-degree elbows. Too many sharp turns reduces water pressure.

YOU'LL NEED

TIME: About four hours to tap into lines and run eight pieces of pipe and their fittings.

SKILLS: Measuring, cutting, and soldering copper pipe.

TOOLS: Hacksaw or tubing cutter, propane torch, groove-joint pliers, adjustable wrench.

1 TAP IN WITH AN ADAPTER.

To go from galvanized to copper or plastic (make sure your locality permits the use of plastic supplies if you choose this option), use a dielectric adapter like the one shown here. Never hook copper pipe directly to galvanized pipe—electrolytic action will corrode the connection.

2 MAKE NEW PIPE CONNECTIONS.

Replace the run with copper or plastic pipe and a tee fitting. Splice with a slip coupling and spacer. Solder or cement the pipes and fittings (see page 142–145, 155). As you install the pipes that lead to the new service, slope the lines slightly so you can easily drain the system.

3 INSTALL DROP ELLS.

At the new fixture, use drop ells instead of regular elbows. Attach them with screws to a piece of wood that is firmly anchored to the framing. Make sure they are positioned 6 to 8 inches apart.

Follow the directions given on pages 142–145 for soldering copper pipes, or see pages 152–155 for cementing plastic pipe. Before soldering copper, open every faucet on the run. Otherwise, heat from the torch can burn out washers and other parts, and built-up steam can rupture a fitting or pipe wall.

Cap the lines, turn on the water, and check for leaks. Don't cover the opening yet; the inspector will want to look at the pipes before you patch the wall.

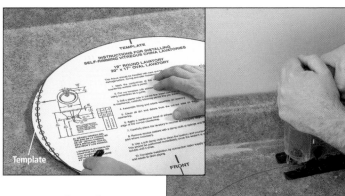

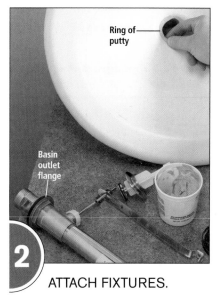

S etting a new sink in place is one of the truly satisfying plumbing tasks. It signals the completion of a fairly easy job that gets noticed immediately.

When shopping for a new rimmed (also known as deck mounted) fixture, you'll find plenty of options—stainless steel, cast-iron, plastic composite, vitreous china, and more. Most kitchen and bath sinks manufactured today are self-rimming, which means installation is as easy as putting some putty on the rim and clamping the sink to the countertop.

To remove an old sink, turn off the supply stops or shut off the water to your house and drain the lines. Disconnect the supply lines and the trap that joins the sink to the drainpipe. Remove mounting clips from underneath and pry up the sink.

1 FOR A BATHROOM SINK, FIRST CUT AN OPENING.

If you need to cut a hole for the sink, trace the template provided with the sink onto the countertop surface. Drill an entry hole and cut using a saber saw and fine-tooth blade.

2 ATTACH FIXTURES.

Before lowering the sink into the opening, hook up the faucet (see pages 42–45) and drain assembly (see page 77). With bathroom sinks, the drain assembly consists of a basin outlet flange, drain body, gasket, locknut, and tailpiece, which slides into the P-trap. (Installing these after you install the sink is difficult, and you also run the risk of damaging the parts.) Lay a bead of plumber's putty around the basin outlet, insert the flange, and screw together the other parts of the drain assembly.

3 SET THE SINK.

Apply a thick bead of silicone adhesive around the underside of the fixture's flange, about ¼ inch from the edge. Turn the sink right side up and lower it carefully into the opening. Press down on the sink; some of the caulk will ooze out. Wipe away the excess. After the silicone adhesive has set (about two hours), apply latex caulk around the sink.

Installing rimmed sinks *(continued)*

Installing stainless-steel sinks

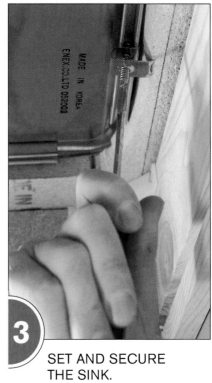

Do not cut this line; cut 1" or so inside it

1 FOR A STAINLESS-STEEL SINK, MARK AND CUT AN OPENING.

Turn your sink upside down on the countertop. Make sure it is in the correct position, safely set back from the cabinet beneath. Trace the outline of the sink, then draw a line that is an inch or so to the inside of that outline. Erase the first line to make sure you do not cut it. Test the sink for fit. Cut the opening using a circular saw with a fine-tooth blade for the straight cuts and a jigsaw for curves. Take your time to avoid splintering the laminate.

2 ATTACH THE FAUCETS AND STRAINER.

Attach a basket strainer to each bowl. Lay a bead of putty around the outlet, set the gasket in place, and lower the strainer body into the hole. With your other hand, from underneath, slip the friction ring in place, and screw on the locknut. Tighten, and clean away the putty that oozes out. You also can attach the tailpiece and trap assembly at this point. To install the faucet, see pages 42–45.

3 SET AND SECURE THE SINK.

To set the sink, first place a rope of plumber's putty all around the rim. Turn the sink right side up, and lower it into the opening. Secure the sink to the countertop with sink clips every 6 to 8 inches. Working from underneath the sink, tighten the clips with a screwdriver. Remove excess putty with a putty knife and a rag dipped in paint thinner.

INSTALL A CAST-IRON SINK.

To set a cast-iron kitchen sink, use the same technique used to set the rimmed sink (see page 99). Run a bead of silicone sealant under the rim, turn the sink right side up, set it in place, and wipe away the excess sealant. Run caulk along the edge and smooth it with a finger.

INSTALLING WALL-MOUNT SINKS

Wall-mount bathroom sinks are not as popular as they once were but remain useful where space is limited or a retro style is called for. Installing the bracket support is a time-consuming part of this job.

YOU'LL NEED

TIME: A half day to add framing and install a new sink (not including drywall patching and painting).

SKILLS: Basic plumbing and carpentry skills.

TOOLS: Keyhole saw, hammer, level, screwdriver, groove-joint pliers or pipe wrench.

Notch studs and anchor a piece of 2 × 10.

1 ROUGH-IN, PROVIDE BRACING.

Be sure to shut off the water and drain the line. To remove an old fixture, disconnect the drain and supply lines. Then look underneath to see if it is held by bolts. If so, loosen or cut the bolts. Pull straight up on the sink to dislodge it.

For a new installation, run new supply lines (see pages 92–98) and provide solid framing for the hanger bracket.

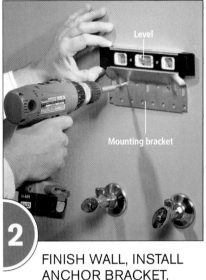

Level

Mounting bracket

2 FINISH WALL, INSTALL ANCHOR BRACKET.

Install the drywall. You may even want to tape and paint it—it will be easier to do now than after the sink is in place. Secure the hanger bracket to the 2×10 blocking. Use plenty of screws and make sure the bracket is level. If they are not already in place, equip each supply line with a stop valve (see pages 20 and 26).

3 SET SINK IN PLACE.

Turn the sink on its side and install the faucet and the drain assembly (see pages 42–45, 68). Attach flexible supply lines to the sink. Hold the sink above the bracket, against the wall, and lower it onto the bracket. A flange fits into a slot in the sink. Have a helper guide the supply tubes into the stop valves.

4 ATTACH LEGS.

If your sink comes with support legs, insert them into the holes in the bottom of the sink, plumb them, and adjust them so they firmly support the sink. To do this, twist the top portion of each leg. Test the sink for level.

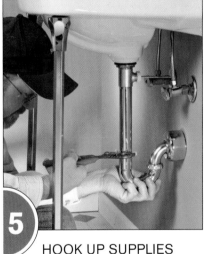

5 HOOK UP SUPPLIES AND DRAIN.

Connect the flexible supply lines to the stop valves. Connect the trap to the sink drain and to the drainpipe. Restore water pressure and check supply lines for leaks. To test the drain for leaks, pull the stopper lever up, fill the bowl, and open the stopper.

ADDING VANITIES

Homeowners love vanities because they add storage capacity in otherwise wasted space. A sink and vanity are easier to install than a wall-hung or pedestal unit because the sink sits on the vanity rather than hanging from the wall. As a result, measurements and cuts can be less exact. Even finishing the wall is simplified. If your vanity has a back panel, you can leave the wall around the plumbing as is—the vanity covers it.

>

STYLE AND STORAGE
Vanities provide even a small bathroom with good-looking, convenient storage.

YOU'LL NEED

TIME: A day to add the vanity and install the basic plumbing.

SKILLS: Basic plumbing and carpentry skills.

TOOLS: Jigsaw, screwdriver, groove-joint pliers, caulk gun.

① INSTALL PLUMBING, CABINET.

Install the supply lines and drain line—make sure they won't interfere with the sink and that the cabinet will cover them. If the cabinet has a back, measure carefully and cut out holes. Slide the cabinet into position and level it from side to side and front to back with shims. Drive screws through the cabinet frame and into studs to anchor it to the wall.

② HOOK UP THE SINK TOP.

Turn the sink top on its side and install the faucet, the flexible supply lines, and the drain assembly. Run a bead of silicone caulk under the sink top to anchor it to the cabinet. Set it on top of the cabinet and make the final connections. Restore water pressure and check for leaks.

INSTALLING PEDESTAL SINKS

Pedestal sinks accomplish what wall-hung sinks do not: They hide the plumbing without a cabinet. However, installation is more difficult than for a regular wall-mount sink or a vanity. You have to get all the plumbing to fit inside the pedestal, and you must attach the sink at the right height so the pedestal fits beneath it. Watch out for less expensive units that have narrower than usual pedestals.

>

ADD ELEGANCE
Pedestal sinks lend an air of elegance. Not for the powder room only, a variety of affordable reproductions fit into large and small bathrooms alike.

YOU'LL NEED

TIME: A day to move the plumbing and install the sink.

SKILLS: Basic plumbing and carpentry skills.

TOOLS: Keyhole saw, hammer or drill, screwdriver, groove-joint pliers.

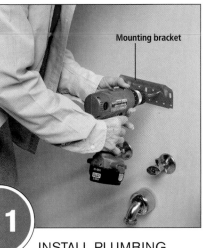

Mounting bracket

1 INSTALL PLUMBING, FRAMING.

Shut off the water. Open the wall and install a 2×10 (see page 101). Measure the width of the pedestal and install the drain and supply lines so they'll fit inside. Finish the walls and install stop valves. Position the sink and pedestal against the wall to mark the bracket's location. Attach the bracket to the wall.

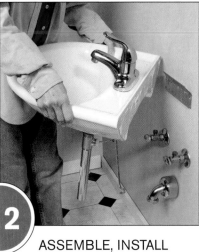

2 ASSEMBLE, INSTALL THE SINK.

Carefully set the sink into the bracket and fasten with the nuts and bolts or toggle bolts provided. Slide the pedestal in and caulk around the bottom with bathtub caulk. Restore water pressure and check for leaks.

CHOOSING PREFAB SHOWER SURROUNDS

A successful shower installation requires careful planning and plenty of work. In most cases, the job calls for three kinds of tasks: framing walls, installing the plumbing, and finishing walls. For information about framing, finishing, and tiling shower stall walls for the projects on this page, refer to books at your local library.

First decide where you would like to put the shower. You need a space at least 32 inches square—36 inches makes for a more comfortable shower—not including the thickness of new walls you may have to build. Be sure to leave room for the shower door to open and close. See pages 86–89 for help in planning.

Next, plan the rough plumbing. The most important issue is how you will vent the unit (see pages 86–88 for options). Make sure you can install a drain line without seriously weakening your joists. The supply lines are easy to plan for—you simply tap into and extend existing lines (see pages 92–93).

Sometimes during new house construction, plumbers install plumbing lines for possible future use. If you're lucky, the drain line you need is poking up through the basement floor. (For installation of a drain line, see page 94.)

The final step in planning a shower is to choose the material the shower is made from. One-, two-, or three-piece prefabricated fiberglass stalls are available. In addition, you can purchase knockdown units, which have a base and walls that you put together; freestanding metal units that don't require framing; and plastic or concrete shower bases with tiled walls.

A variety of glass doors are available, or you can hang a shower curtain.

PREFAB SHOWER STALLS.

Prefabricated stalls usually come with a base, as well as framing instructions. A freestanding one-piece unit is the easiest to install but may be too bulky to haul into your bathroom. When logistics require, use a multipiece unit. Other options include a freestanding metal unit, usually installed in basements as utility showers. Or you may choose to construct tiled walls around a shower base. Tile also offers wide color options.

TIPS FOR PLANNING A NEW SHOWER

- For a coordinated look, choose the whole ensemble at once: door, stall or tile, base, and faucet and showerhead.

- Unless you have better-than-average ventilation or live in an extra-dry area, install a bathroom vent fan near the shower. A shower introduces a great deal of moisture that could damage walls and lead to mildew problems if not properly vented.

- Consider hiring a professional to install the shower base with drain and vent. Installing the showerhead and controls and finishing the walls are comparatively easy tasks.

- Although 32-inch bases and prefab units are available, most adults feel cramped in them. If possible, install a 36-inch base.

INSTALLING A SHOWER SURROUND

A preformed fiberglass shower enclosure is a convenient alternative to waiting in line to use the shower. Easier and faster to install than tiling a shower, the process is well within the abilities of the average do-it-yourselfer. If the base and plumbing are already in place, you can complete the shower installation over the weekend.

Measure the space for the shower. You will want to purchase the largest enclosure that will fit the available space. Avoid installing an enclosure that's smaller than 3 foot square. Elbow room is a necessity, and a shower that is too small will not get used.

INSULATE TO REDUCE NOISE

Packing the walls of a shower with insulation reduces the tin-roof sound of water against the thin shower walls.

YOU'LL NEED

TIME: About two days; one day to install and one to allow the adhesive to dry before use.

SKILLS: Carpentry skills, basic plumbing skills, using adhesives.

TOOLS: Tape measure, carpenter's level, utility knife, straightedge, pencil, caulking gun, power drill, carbide holesaw, adjustable wrench.

PREFABRICATED ENCLOSURES
Fiberglass shower units are an easy alternative compared to the work involved in constructing a tiled shower. Choices vary from very narrow units to spacious enclosures.

SIMPLE ELEGANCE
Prefabricated shower stalls are available in a variety of shapes and colors to fit virtually any bathroom style and floor plan.

PREPARE THE WALLS.

Cover the framing with greenboard (moisture resistant drywall) or cement backerboard. This is particularly important for areas near the enclosure; they will often get wet. Tape, then prime or seal the walls before installing the panels. If you're working in an existing shower area, shut off the water supply and remove any handles. An enclosure can be installed onto wall tiles as long as you clean and rinse them thoroughly, to ensure that the adhesive will stick. Finish cleaning using denatured alcohol.

Installing a shower surround *(continued)*

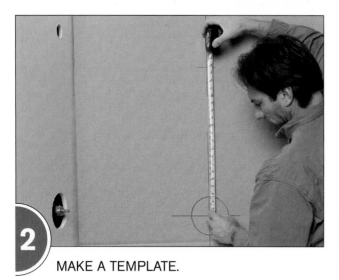

② MAKE A TEMPLATE.

First, install the side panel with the plumbing cutouts. To ensure against cutting mistakes—which cannot be corrected— make a template using a large piece of cardboard (the shipping carton is a good source). Measure over from the wall and up from the shower pan to locate the center of each hole and transfer those measurements to the template. Use a compass to draw circles the size of the openings. Cut the template and test it for fit. Correct any mistakes using scrap cardboard pieces and masking tape.

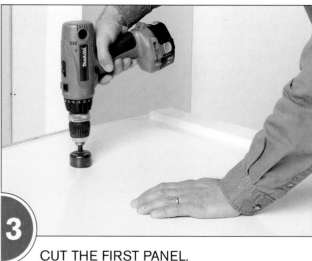

③ CUT THE FIRST PANEL.

Lay the panel on a flat surface and place the template on top. Use masking tape to hold the template's edges flush with the panel's edges. Use a pencil or felt-tipped marker to scribe the cutout lines. Drill smaller holes using a holesaw. You may need a jigsaw for a larger hole. The holes should be large enough to accommodate the plumbing, but small enough for the escutcheons (flanges) to completely cover the hole. Test-fit the panel; you may need to trim it.

④ AFFIX THE FIRST PANEL.

Use a caulk gun to apply squiggles of manufacturer-recommended adhesive to the back of the panel. Be sure to apply adhesive to the edges as well as the middle of the panel. Set the panel on the base, align it, then arch it against the wall, gently pressing it into place as you go. Once you are sure it is correctly positioned, press more firmly. Pull the panel back a few inches and wait a minute or so for the adhesive to begin to set up. Press the panel back in place. Once you are sure it is correctly positioned, press and run your hands from side to side as well as up and down until it is firmly attached to the wall at all points.

⑤ AFFIX THE REMAINING PANELS.

The remaining panels may not need to be cut. Test each for fit, then adhere them as described in step 4.

Installing a tub and shower riser requires both plumbing and carpentry skills. And, if you decide to install a whirlpool tub (see pages 109–112), you'll need basic electric wiring skills as well. Sketch an installation drawing of your layout first, then use the drawing to make a tool and materials list.

If replacing an old riser, check for water damage. Include the removal and replacement of damaged or deteriorated subflooring or studs in your plan.

Design a new riser to fit the existing riser holes and blocking for an upgraded project. If the installation involves new construction, you'll need to drill riser holes in the subflooring and install blocking.

For a new installation, decide where you want to place the tub. Locate the nearest water supply. Measure and sketch the run from the existing water supply.

Installing or upgrading a bathroom riser typically requires a permit. Follow the local codes, and ask your residential building inspector what inspection steps need to be taken during the construction process. Call the local building inspector to make an appointment to inspect the work at each point. Have the inspector sign off on the work before you cover up any work.

YOU'LL NEED

TIME: About 6 to 8 hours.

SKILLS: Carpentry skills, connecting plumbing fixtures, soldering.

TOOLS: Tape measure, carpenter's level, propane torch, striker, soldering kit, tubing cutter, hammer, power drill, bits, screwdriver.

1 DRILL FOR THE RISER.

Determine the best location to tap into supply lines (see pages 92–93). Drill two holes at least ¼ inch larger than the diameter of the riser pipe through the stud wall into the subfloor. The extra permits some flexibility when hooking up the supply lines. The type of fixture you buy determines the distance between the hot and cold supply risers. Refer to the faucet manufacturer's instructions for placement of the risers.

2 INSTALL BLOCKING.

Center the tub spout blocking 4 inches above the top of the tub. Install a separate blocking for the faucets, if placing them more than 6 inches above the spout. Make sure that the blocking is level, at the manufacturer's specified depth inside the wall. Toenail it firmly to the studs. The height of the showerhead blocking depends on what suits your needs. The standard height for showerheads is 6 feet, 6 inches above the floor.

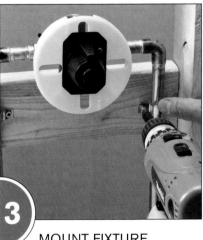

3 MOUNT FIXTURE ASSEMBLY.

Measure and record on a drawing the lengths needed for the risers, integral stops, and tub spout. Cut the pieces to the specified lengths. Mount the fixture assembly on the blocking. Make sure it is centered and level. Connect the adapters using plumber's tape or plumbing compound.

4 TEST-FIT PIPE RUN.

Assemble the copper tubing and fittings for the riser to test-fit the run. Make sure all the pieces fit. Double-check faucet controls to make sure they're centered and level. Make necessary adjustments before soldering.

Installing a tub and shower riser *(continued)*

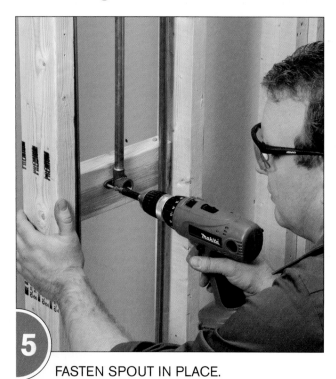

5 FASTEN SPOUT IN PLACE.

Solder the copper fittings (see pages 142–145). Attach the spout.

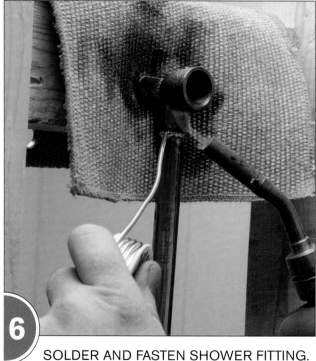

6 SOLDER AND FASTEN SHOWER FITTING.

Solder the piping for the showerhead. Secure it to the blocking.

7 CONNECT TO SUPPLY LINE.

Before connecting the riser to the supply lines, find out if the inspector wants to have the lines tested. Otherwise connect the supply risers to the supply lines. Turn on the water and check for leaks.

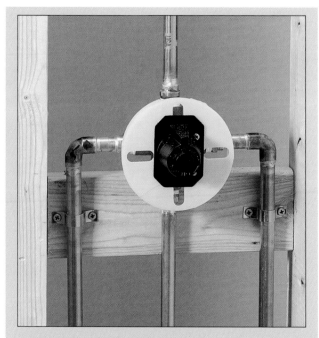

TYPES OF SUPPLY RISERS.

Three types of supply risers are available: single-handle, two-handle, and three-handle. The two- and three-handle faucets have either compression or cartridge valves. Single-handle faucet designs vary among cartridge, ball-type, or disc.

INSTALLING A BATHTUB

The bathtub has become the major focal point in a bathroom design. Before beginning the hunt for the perfect bathtub, take note of your household members' bathing habits. A whirlpool tub might be attractive, but a standard tub-shower combination with accessories such as a seat or multiple showerheads may be the more logical choice.

Address installation issues before buying and having the tub delivered. A standard tub measures 60 inches long by 30 inches wide and holds about 50 gallons of water. The benefit of installing a standard-size tub is that it's not too difficult to get it up a flight of stairs.

Luxury soaking tubs and whirlpools require a more creative approach to transport to a second-floor bathroom. Their size and bulk may make it impossible to negotiate the stairs. You may have to consider pulling out a window or opening a wall to hoist the tub into the bathroom. Stairs can also be problematic if the tub comes with a built-in enclosure. One way to avoid such problems is to buy a multipiece unit.

Tubs without enclosures give you two choices for apron placement: either left-end aprons or right-end aprons. Your choice of which to purchase is based on faucet placement. If you can't decide which one you want, a tub with a reversible apron gives you the flexibility to decide later. Faucets and fittings are always purchased separately.

Half-inch supply pipes make filling an oversize tub a time-consuming task. When installing the control risers and supply line (see pages 107–108), consider installing ¾-inch supply lines. Also, your old water heater may have served you well in the past, but pair it with a larger tub and the result is tepid bathwater. Keep in mind that tubs with capacities of up to 80 gallons require a 50- to 75-gallon water heater. If a new water heater is not a consideration, purchase a tub that has an in-line heater. These heaters are installed with spa heads so they recirculate bathwater continually, maintaining a consistent temperature.

Most residential bathroom floors are constructed to support the weight of a standard bathtub. Some custom homes will accommodate oversize tubs. Determine whether you need to beef up the floor joists to support an oversize tub or whirlpool.

Removing the old tub

1 DISCONNECT THE DRAIN.

Loosen the screws on the overflow plate and remove it. Pull out the trip lever and linkage. Remove the strainer. Unscrew the drain piece with a pair of pliers and a screwdriver. Pull out the stopper with the linkage attached.

2 CUT THE WALL AWAY.

If the existing wall is tiled, chisel into the grout and pry off at least one course of tile along the edge of the tub. Cut away the wall to reveal the tub flange. Remove the screws or nails that fasten the flange to the studs or ledger.

3 REMOVE THE TUB.

You may be able to pry the tub loose, depending on how it was installed. Pull the tub away from the wall. Have a helper assist you with removing and disposing of it.

Installing a bathtub *(continued)*

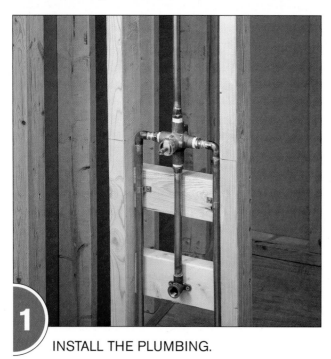

1 INSTALL THE PLUMBING.

If you need to frame new walls for the tub, frame them so the alcove opening is just large enough to slide the tub into place. Leave a gap of ⅛ inch or less at the head and foot of the tub. Install plumbing for the risers, faucet, and showerhead (see pages 107–108). Make sure you install an access panel so you can get to the valves in case of an emergency.

2 LEVEL THE TUB.

Slide the tub into the alcove to test-fit. Set some old blankets or towels, or the shipping cardboard, over the tub floor to protect the bottom of the tub. A dropped tool can do major damage to a tub. Check the tub for level with a carpenter's level. Shim to level. Stay away from using wood shims because they rot when exposed to moisture. The best shims are flattened copper tubing or plastic shims. Mark the location of the top of the nailing flange at each stud. Remove the tub.

3 MARK FOR THE LEDGER.

The ledger board helps support the tub. You'll need to determine the proper height for it by measuring the depth of the nailing flange. Measure this distance down from the previous mark on each stud and make a second mark. These marks serve as a guide for placing the top ledger board.

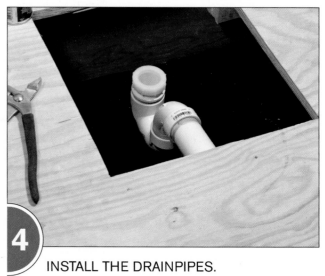

4 INSTALL THE DRAINPIPES.

If the drainpipe and P-trap are not already roughed in, you need to install them. Cut a 4- to 9-inch-wide access hole that extends 12 inches from the center of the end wall in the subfloor. Connect a 1½-inch P-trap. Install a slip nut fitting centered directly under the overflow pipe location of the tub.

5 INSTALL THE LEDGER BOARD.

Cut and drive wood screws or galvanized nails to mount the ledger boards into the wall studs at the marks you made earlier. Some tubs require additional support braces; you may need to adjust the ledger board lengths. Check the ledger boards for level before installing the tub.

6 CONNECT THE OVERFLOW.

Trim the drainpipe as specified in the tub manufacturer's instructions so it will fit the overflow kit. The drainpipe should seat snugly into the pressure fitting on the P-trap. You may have to trim the pipe so it fits. Connect the overflow and drain to the tub. Follow the manufacturer's instructions for connecting the drain and overflow assembly on the tub.

7 INSTALL THE TUB.

Set the tub on the ledgers. The tub must sit firmly against the ledger boards, and the tub drain must fit snugly into the P-trap. Drive galvanized nails through the predrilled holes in the ledger. If there are no predrilled holes, use the nailheads to anchor the tub to the studs.

8 INSERT THE DRAIN LINKAGE.

Snake the drain linkage through the overflow opening. Attach the overflow coverplate and the drain assembly. Test the system for leaks. Before you finish the walls and installation, schedule an inspection. Don't enclose walls prior to inspection, or you may be required to tear out some of your work.

9 COMPLETE THE INSTALLATION.

Finish the tub walls. Install the fixtures. Seal around the faucet handles and tub spout with a good-quality tub-and-tile caulk. Apply a bead of caulk around the edge of the tub. Use your finger to smooth the caulk. Turn on the water and check for leaks. Wait at least 24 hours before using the tub to allow caulking to dry.

INSTALLING A WHIRLPOOL TUB

At a home center or bathroom specialty store, you can find a wide variety of whirlpools (also called spas). If you choose the right model and plan carefully, installing a whirlpool is within the capabilities of a do-it-yourselfer.

Choosing a whirlpool.

Many large units with molded fiberglass sides and a deck can be installed almost as quickly as a standard tub, since they require little framing and no tiling. Some smaller whirlpools are designed to fit in the same space as a standard tub (though they are typically a bit wider). A drop-in model, as shown on these two pages, calls for more planning and work, but it allows you to be creative in designing the surrounding space.

Some models come with their own spout and handles. This eases the installation quite a bit.

Choose a unit that has an integral heating unit, to keep the water hot for as long as you want.

If you'd like to install a large whirlpool, make sure that it will fit through your doors. Some models are so large that they can only be

CUTTING THE OPENING.

Frame the walls out of 2×4s and cut a plywood deck to fit. Use a cardboard template (which may be supplied by the manufacturer) to mark for cutting the hole. Also drill holes for the handles and the spout.

installed in new construction, before the walls are completely framed.

If you will use the whirlpool only as a soaking tub, you need only a tub spout, and a shower door is strictly optional. Most whirlpools can be used as showers, but you must install a shower faucet and a door or a curtain.

Installation considerations

Read the manufacturer's literature before you purchase a whirlpool, so you fully understand the installation requirements.

Plumbing a whirlpool is often not much more complicated than plumbing a standard tub. With most units, you need supply only one hot- and one cold-water line, plus a drain. The whirlpool comes with supply tubes for the jets already installed.

The drain line must be positioned accurately, so you can make the connection with the tub while reaching into the space from outside. Depending on the design, the spout

and control handles may be run through knockout holes in the whirlpool itself, or they may be installed on the surrounding deck or on the wall.

You will need to provide a code-approved electrical receptacle at the proper location. In most cases, the receptacle must be GFCI protected. The receptacle should be accessible after the tub is installed.

The plumbing should be accessible as well. As with a standard tub, you should install access panels so you can reach the drain line and the shutoff valves. You also must provide access to the whirlpool's working parts—especially the pump—to make possible future maintenance and repairs.

Because they are made of flexible fiberglass or acrylic, many whirlpools should be set in a bed of wet mortar. The mortar firms the floor of the whirlpool, so it won't flex when you stand on it.

TUB INSTALLATION MISTAKES

Avoid the mistakes that commonly occur during tub installation:

- Violating or ignoring local code restrictions regarding drain and supply lines, as well as the electrical receptacle.

- Undersizing the pipes.

- Attaching copper to galvanized without a brass or dielectric fitting.

- Failing to wrap pipes with plumber's tape, or using pipe compound at threaded joints.

- Failing to level the whirlpool.

Installing a whirlpool with a custom surround.

With the whirlpool on site so you can check dimensions as you work, build the framing for the surround. Take into account the thickness of the backerboard and tiles that will be installed onto the framing. Also keep in mind that the bottom of the tub should rest on a bed of mortar, which raises it up an inch or so.

Build the frame out of 2x4s, then add a plywood deck. Cut out a hole for the whirlpool, and test that it fits. Remove the tub and run the plumbing lines. Test-fit the whirlpool again to make sure that the drain lines up.

Pour a mortar bed onto the subfloor, set the whirlpool in place, and connect the drain. Once the mortar has set, tile the surround and install the spout and the handles.

GETTING THE FIT RIGHT.

In most cases, the whirlpool's lip should be supported all around the perimeter of the tub, and the bottom should rest in a bed of mortar. Use temporary spacers to keep the lip raised slightly, so you can slip tiles under it.

INSTALLING ANTI-SCALD DEVICES

Anti-scald devices are an important feature to consider if you have small children in your household. Hot tap water accounts for a quarter of the scald burns that require hospitalization among children 4 years and under. Small children do not perceive danger, have less control of their environment, and have a limited ability to react.

Anti-scald devices help prevent these situations by regulating water temperature. Many communities have local codes that require new construction to install devices that maintain water temperatures at or below 120 degrees and prevent sudden changes in water temperature.

You can install these devices yourself. However, if you're considering installing a whole-house device, it's recommended that you hire a professional.

WATER SAFETY.

If you have small children in your home, you need to consider using anti-scald devices for all faucets and showerheads.

KEEP YOUR FAMILY SAFE

- Never leave a small child alone in a bathroom or kitchen. Take the child with you if you must leave the room.

- Set the water heater thermostat to 120°F or less. The lower the setting, the lower the risk of scald-burn related injuries.

- Install anti-scald devices on bathtub faucets and showerheads.

- Always check the water temperature before placing a child in the bathtub or shower. Hold your whole hand in the water and spread your fingers wide. Move your hand back and forth through the water for several seconds checking for hot spots or surges.

INSTALLING HAND SHOWERS

A hand shower attached to an existing shower is a luxurious addition to a shower/tub area. A hand shower attached to a tub faucet is an economical alternative to installing a complete shower, sparing you the trouble of cutting open walls and installing new plumbing.

A variety of designs range from the simple to the exotic. Installing them is quick and easy—a straightforward bathroom upgrade well within the skill level of do-it-yourselfers.

YOU'LL NEED

TIME: An hour or two for either installation.

SKILLS: No special skills needed.

TOOLS: Screwdriver, groove-joint pliers, drill, hammer, awl.

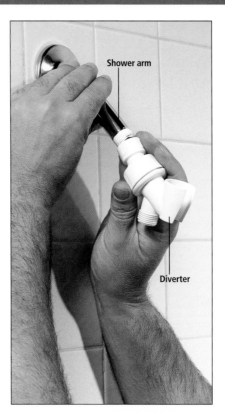

Shower arm

Diverter

AT AN EXISTING SHOWER.

Use pliers to remove the showerhead. Tape the jaws of the pliers to protect chrome parts from scratches. Clean the threads. If your shower arm doesn't have male threads, replace it with one that does. Wrap the threads with plumber's tape and screw on the hand shower with pliers. The hand shower connector may have a diverter (which allows you to choose either the fixed or the hand-held head), a hanger bracket (the new head fits on it), or a direct hose hookup (the hose attaches to the shower arm). For the latter, install a shower hanger (below).

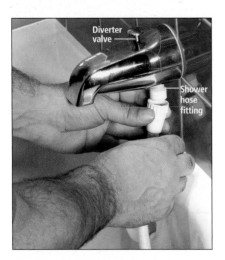

Diverter valve

Shower hose fitting

A TUB-ONLY UNIT.

To remove the old spout, insert the handle of a hammer or pliers into the spout opening and turn counterclockwise. Clean the pipe threads. You may need to remove the existing nipple and install one that is longer or shorter. Apply plumber's tape and screw on the new spout with a diverter valve. Attach the hose to the shower-hose fitting.

Mark screw holes

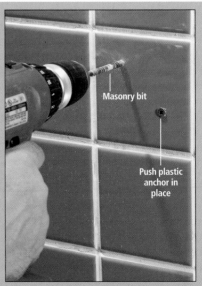

Masonry bit

Push plastic anchor in place

MOUNT THE SHOWER HANGER.

Some hangers have self-sticking backs. You simply peel off the paper backs and stick them in place. Be sure the wall is absolutely clean and dry before doing so. For a more permanent installation, hold the hanger in position and mark the screw holes. With a hammer and an awl or nail, tap a little nick into the tile—gently, so you don't crack the tile. The nick will keep your masonry bit from slipping on the ceramic glaze as you start the hole. Drill the holes, push plastic anchors in place, and secure the hanger with screws.

CHOOSING WATER SOFTENERS

A water softener removes minerals (especially iron, calcium, and magnesium) from water by means of ion exchange. As water passes through the unit, minerals are absorbed and replaced with sodium, which comes from salt that you must add to the storage tank from time to time.

The resulting soft water cleans clothes better than mineral-laden hard water, which creates fewer suds. The drawback is that it adds salt to the water—probably not enough to damage your health, but enough to affect the taste of the water.

It is best to have a cold water bypass so some faucets receive unsoftened cold water. At least make sure your toilets and outside sill cocks do not receive softened water, or you will be paying for a lot of extra salt.

In most cases, it pays to have a water softener service install and maintain your water softener. If you were to install one yourself, you would have to make drain and electrical connections, then periodically flush and recharge your system. With a service unit, the dealer simply brings a fresh tank and takes the old one to regenerate it.

In the unit shown, a bypass valve lets you or the dealer service the unit without shutting down your home's water supply.

FILTERING BACTERIA

If bacteria in the water is a problem rather than simply minerals, sediment, taste, or odor, choose a filter carefully. Some filters actually increase the amount of bacteria in your drinking water because they remove chlorine. Bacteria can grow in dechlorinated water if it sits for a while, even if it's in your refrigerator.

Water that is "hard" is laced with minerals such as calcium and iron. Hard water inhibits the cleaning power of soap and detergent, and also makes rinsing difficult, so you end up with soapy buildup in sinks and tubs. It creates reddish iron stains or collections of white mineral deposits, which can clog faucets and pipes.

Through a process called ion exchange, a water softener removes most of the minerals and replaces them with trace amounts of sodium salt). The resulting water cleans well and will not harm plumbing, but may taste bad.

If you have hard water, it is a neighborhood-wide problem (unless you get your water from your own well). Consult with a plumbing expert at a local hardware store or home center to find the best solution.

The easiest solution is to have a water softener company install and maintain a softener. However, you can save money if you install one yourself. Maintenance involves adding salt periodically and occasionally cleaning a line and a screen.

You can install a water softener on the main water supply line where it enters your house. Or, install it on the hot-water pipe that leaves the water heater; that way, your cold water will taste better.

YOU'LL NEED

TIME: 4 to 6 hours.

SKILLS: Working with copper pipe, using basic plumbing tools, connecting fittings.

TOOLS: Adjustable wrench, screwdriver, tape measure, solder, flux, propane torch, deburring tool, emery cloth.

ASSEMBLE AND POSITION THE SOFTENER.

Place the water softener near the main supply line or a hot-water pipe, in a spot where you can easily reach it for adding salt. Follow manufacturer's instructions for assembling the unit. Attach the drain hose and the overflow tube, and run them to a point that is at least 1½ inches above a floor drain or a utility tub drain. Check that the softener is stable and level; you may need to shim the bottom of the unit.

INSTALL THE BYPASS VALVE.

The softener comes with a bypass valve, which you must assemble and install. In most cases, you simply slip on O-rings, push the valves into the ports, and attach the valves with push-on clips. Be sure to lubricate the O-rings as recommended by the manufacturer.

Turn off the water at the main house supply valve (or to the pipe you are breaking into), and open a nearby faucet to drain the line. Shut off gas or electricity to the water heater.

CONNECTING THE WATER SUPPLY.

Near the water softener, break into the supply pipe. Remove a section of pipe about 5 inches long. Install elbows and pipes that reach to the bypass valves. The valves typically accept ¾-inch pipe. If the pipe is larger, use reducer couplings or reducer elbows to make the transition.

Local codes may require that you configure the pipes so that the water can bypass the softener when repairs are needed. This typically involves using tees rather than elbows, and installing three shutoff valves.

Do all your soldering while the pipe is not touching the bypass valves, or you could damage them. Run copper pipes down into the bypass valves. The final connection

is typically made using a coupler that is supplied by the manufacturer.

Remove aerators and showerheads throughout the house, and run water for several minutes. Turn off the faucets and replace the aerators and heads. Follow the manufacturer's instructions for programming the softener.

INSTALLING WATER FILTRATION SYSTEMS

If you receive municipal water, you'll find information concerning water quality at city hall. If you have a well, you're on your own. Your local department of health can recommend a company to test your water to see if you need a filter. A test for bacteria is relatively inexpensive, but a full test that includes a search for pesticides, organic matter, and other potential problems is costly. Ask local officials if other people in your area have had similar tests done and what, if any, contaminants were found.

If the taste of your drinking water is your major concern, try a faucet filter before you get involved with a more expensive installation. If you have mineral-laden hard water, install a water softener (see pages 115–116).

WATER FILTRATION OPTIONS

Sediment	This option uses a filter to screen out particles that clog your aerators and make your water look cloudy. Usually a sediment filter is used in conjunction with an activated-charcoal filter.
Activated-charcoal	This filter removes organic chemicals and pesticides. If your water is heavily chlorinated, it will remove much of the chlorine and improve the taste of your water. If taste is your major concern, install a unit at the kitchen spout. Whole-house units require you to change the charcoal filter fairly frequently.
Reverse osmosis	This is the most extreme measure, capable of removing bacteria and harmful chemicals. It is expensive and bulky, and requires at least one holding tank. You can combine this system with an activated-charcoal system installed near the kitchen sink.
Water softener	Also called an ion-exchange unit, this system greatly reduces minerals such as calcium and iron. Have a water softener company install one for you—the required piping is specialized and complicated.

INSTALLING WHOLE-HOUSE SYSTEMS

This typical whole-house system combines a sediment filter with an activated-charcoal unit. The plumbing is not complicated, but you'll have to shut off water to the whole house before beginning. You also may have to reroute or raise pipes in order to gain enough room to install the two units.

YOU'LL NEED

TIME: Half a day.

SKILLS: Good plumbing skills.

TOOLS: Wrenches and pliers; propane torch, if you need to solder copper pipe.

Shut off the water and drain the line. At a convenient point near the outlet side of the water meter (or just inside the house, if you have no meter), break into the line by opening a union or cutting the pipe (see pages 150, 92–93). Install a shutoff valve if you don't have one (see page 26). Remove 4 feet of pipe and work toward the meter. If you wish, add a stop valve to cut off backflow when you need to change filters. Then install the charcoal filter, a nipple, and finally the sediment filter. Make the last joint with a union or sleeve coupling.

A whole-house filtration system will supply you with filtered water in every tap and likely will prolong the life of your water-using appliances. But because it is fairly difficult to install and requires regular filter changes, most homeowners opt to go without. They reason that most water does not need to be treated because it is used for bathing, flushing away waste, and washing clothes. Instead, they choose to filter the water that counts most: their drinking and cooking water.

You can install a unit that gives you filtered water every time you turn on the cold water at your kitchen sink, or you can install a separate faucet with the filter. The first type saves you the trouble of drilling a hole and installing a separate faucet. The separate faucet (installed much like the hot water dispenser on page 125) means you'll change filter cartridges less often.

Some systems include an activated-charcoal filter. This two-canister system takes more time to install but adds another stage of filtration.

Before you purchase a unit, measure the space under your sink to make sure the new unit will fit. The connectors for the various types available are fairly simple, ranging from standard compression fittings to simple connectors designed to quickly attach to flexible supply lines. In most cases, you need only shut off the cold water supply, cut into a flexible supply, and install the system.

YOU'LL NEED

TIME: Usually 30 minutes.

SKILLS: Basic plumbing skills.

TOOLS: Tubing cutter, flashlight, screwdriver.

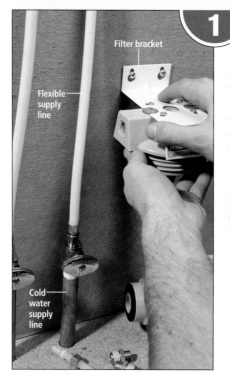

Filter bracket

Flexible supply line

Cold water supply line

1 FILTERING THE COLD WATER TAP.

Anchor the filter in a location that's easy to get at when it's time to replace the filter cartridge. Allow enough clearance underneath to unscrew the canister. Use the screws provided to fasten it to the cabinet back or wall. If you don't have a flexible cold water supply line, install one (see page 146). Cut into the cold water supply using a tubing cutter or plastic tubing cutter.

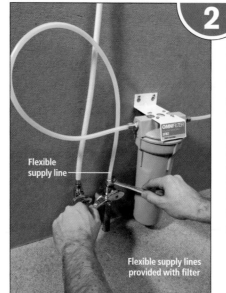

Flexible supply line

Flexible supply lines provided with filter

2 HOOK UP THE FILTER.

Note which filter inlet is marked for the incoming supply and connect that flexible tube to the section of supply line nearest the shutoff valve. Connectors vary. For the ones shown, simply push the tubing in and they're joined. Connect the tube that carries filtered water to the section of flexible supply line for the faucet. Follow the manufacturer's directions for lubricating the canister seal and using the system.

PLUMBING ICEMAKERS

If you have just purchased a new refrigerator with an icemaker, the appliance dealer may offer installation for a minimal cost. If not, installing an icemaker yourself is usually not a difficult project.

If you would like to add an icemaker to an older refrigerator, contact an appliance dealer to see if you can buy and install a retrofit unit.

If you have hard or bad-tasting water, consider installing a small water filter for the icemaker. You will likely need to change the filter cartridge once a year or so.

Use copper tubing, as shown on this page, or plastic tubing. Plastic is less likely to kink, making it a good choice if you plan to move the refrigerator often. However, plastic tubing clogs more easily than copper tubing.

Here we show installing a saddle-tee valve, which is usually reliable. For a sturdier installation, you may choose to install a stop valve instead.

Twist handle clockwise to seat valve

1 INSTALL A SADDLE-TEE VALVE.

Find a cold-water pipe that is near the refrigerator and that can be accessed for future maintenance. To install a self-punching model, simply position the rubber seal under the punch and tighten the clamp screws. Twist the valve until it pokes through. To install a more reliable type of saddle valve, shut off water and drill a hole in the pipe before clamping the valve.

2 RUN THE TUBING.

Purchase plenty of tubing, so you can run it around in gentle curves and so you can provide loops that allow the refrigerator to be moved in and out. On the floor behind the refrigerator and near the base molding, use a drill with a long bit to bore a hole through to the basement or crawlspace below. Or, drill a hole near the bottom of a wall to reach an adjacent room. Carefully uncoil the tubing; if it gets kinked, the whole piece must be replaced. Thread the tubing through the hole and run it to the saddle valve. Behind the refrigerator, leave several coils of tubing. Take care not to squeeze a tubing end, or it will not fit into the compression fitting.

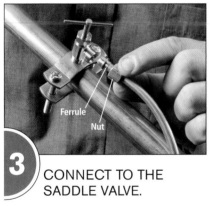

Ferrule
Nut

3 CONNECT TO THE SADDLE VALVE.

Bend the tubing so its end will run straight into the saddle valve's fitting. Slip on a nut and a ferrule, poke the tubing in, and tighten the nut.

4 CONNECT TO THE REFRIGERATOR.

Place the other end of the tubing in a bucket and turn on the saddle valve. Run water for a minute or so to purge the line of debris. Turn off the saddle-tee valve. At the refrigerator's icemaker connection, attach the tubing as you did at the saddle valve (step 3). Open the saddle valve and check for leaks; you may need to tighten a nut.

SADDLE VALVES

Choose from two types of saddle valves. A self-punching saddle valve drives a spike that punctures the copper water supply pipe, allowing you to add the new water line without shutting off the water supply. Simply clamp it in place and twist the valve handle until the spike punctures the pipe. The second type requires you to drill a hole through the water supply line, twist the valve into the hole, and clamp it firmly to the water supply pipe.

YOU'LL NEED

TIME: Usually 30 minutes.

SKILLS: Basic plumbing skills.

TOOLS: Tubing cutter, adjustable wrench, flashlight, screwdriver.

INSTALLING GARBAGE DISPOSERS

A garbage disposer is a useful kitchen upgrade that isn't too difficult to install. The hardest part is working under your sink, so pad the cabinet with plenty of towels to make it comfortable. If you're installing a new sink, attach the disposer to the sink first, then set the sink in place. Begin by removing the trap from one of the sink strainers.

YOU'LL NEED

TIME: Several hours, not including the electrical receptacle and switch.

SKILLS: Basic electrical and plumbing connections.

TOOLS: Hammer, spud wrench, screwdriver, groove-joint pliers, putty knife, wire stripper.

1 SUPPLY ELECTRICITY.

If necessary, install an electrical box under the sink near the disposer. Install a GFCI receptacle. Or you can hard-wire the disposer (see Step 6 on page 121). Unless you are using a self-switching disposer, install a switch as well.

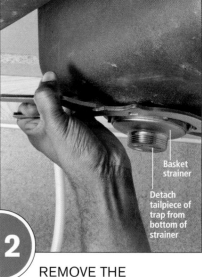

Basket strainer

Detach tailpiece of trap from bottom of strainer

2 REMOVE THE BASKET STRAINER.

Disconnect the trap assembly from the basket strainer and the drainpipe. Remove the locknut that holds the strainer in place using a spud wrench or a hammer and screwdriver, as shown. Lift out the strainer and clean away old putty from around the sink opening using a putty knife, paint thinner, and an abrasive pad.

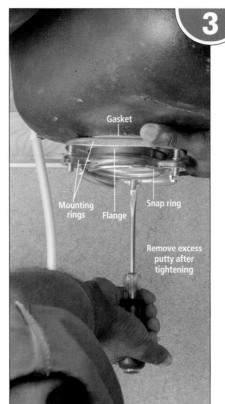

Gasket

Mounting rings   Flange   Snap ring

Remove excess putty after tightening

3 INSTALL THE MOUNTING ASSEMBLY.

First take apart the mounting assembly. To do this, remove the snap ring, mounting rings, and gasket from the flange. Then lay a rope of putty around the sink opening and seat the flange in the opening. Have a helper hold the flange in place as you work from underneath. Slip the gasket, mounting rings, and snap ring onto the flange. The snap ring will keep the mounting assembly in place temporarily. Tighten the mounting assembly against the sink by turning the screws counterclockwise, as shown. Tighten each screw a little at a time to assure a solid seal. With a putty knife, shave away excess putty.

Connect black to black, white to white, and ground to green screw

Ground

④ CONNECT THE ELECTRICAL CORD.

Remove the disposer's electrical coverplate. Strip sheathing and wire insulation from an approved appliance cord and insert the cord into the opening. Tighten the clamp while holding the cord in place. Make the electrical connections in the disposer, gently push the wires into place, and reinstall the coverplate.

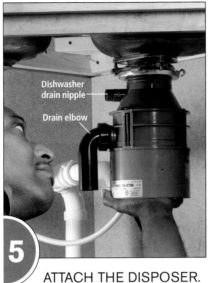

Dishwasher drain nipple

Drain elbow

⑤ ATTACH THE DISPOSER.

Secure the drain elbow to the disposer. If you'll drain a dishwasher through the unit, remove the knockout inside the nipple. To mount the disposer, lift it into place and rotate it until it engages and tightens. (This may take some muscle.) Once the connection is made, rotate the disposer to the best position for attaching the drain lines.

⑥ MAKE THE ELECTRICAL CONNECTION.

Shut off power. If you installed an electrical receptacle, simply insert the disposer's plug. For a hard-wired installation, connect the source black wire to the switch black wire, the white switch wire to the black wire that leads to the disposer, the white disposer wire to the white power source wire, and all the ground wires together.

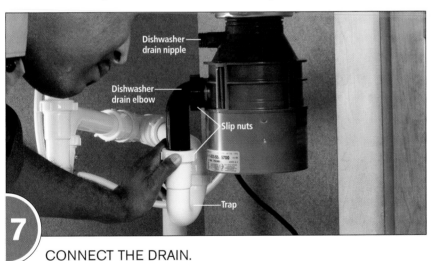

Dishwasher drain nipple

Dishwasher drain elbow

Slip nuts

Trap

⑦ CONNECT THE DRAIN.

Fit a slip nut and a rubber washer onto the drain elbow and fasten the trap to the elbow and the drainpipe. You may need to cut the elbow to make the connection. For double sinks, connect the elbow to the second bowl drain. If you will be draining a dishwasher through the disposer, connect the dishwasher drain hose to the drain nipple of the disposer. Use an automotive clamp to attach the hose, tightening it in place with a screwdriver or ratchet and socket. Run water down through the disposer to test for leaks. Turn the electrical power back on. With standing water in the bowl, turn the disposer on and make sure it is securely attached.

TIPS ON INSTALLING THE DRAINPIPES

With double-bowl sinks, it's possible to remove the disposer's drain elbow and run pipe straight to the trap of the other bowl. It's better, however, to install a separate trap for the disposer so each bowl has its own trap.

If the original drain traps are in good condition, reuse them. In most cases, if you buy one extension piece, you will have enough material to complete the piping. If your old trap looks at all worn, replace it while you have everything apart.

MAINTAINING GARBAGE DISPOSERS

To avoid maintenance problems, be sure you have cold water running before you turn on your disposer. Gradually feed in food waste and don't stick a spatula or spoon past the splash guard. With the cold water continuing to flow, run the disposer for a few seconds after the food has been ground. If you hear a clanking sound, switch off or unplug the disposer and remove the object that has caused the problem.

REMOVE STUCK OBJECTS

If any solid object gets past the splash guard, it can cause the disposer to jam. If this happens, turn off the power (it may have shut itself off). Remove the splash guard and look into the disposer with a flashlight. If you can't free the object, rotate the grinder with a broom handle or turning tool.

CAUTION

DON'T USE CHEMICALS

Don't attempt to clear a blocked drain line with chemicals of any kind—not even "safe" chemicals. If the solution doesn't work, you'll be in danger of getting spattered with it when you try to clear the line.

YOU'LL NEED

TIME: Less than an hour to deal with most problems.

SKILLS: No special skills needed, unless you need to auger.

TOOLS: Allen wrench or disposer turning tool, flashlight, auger, broom handle.

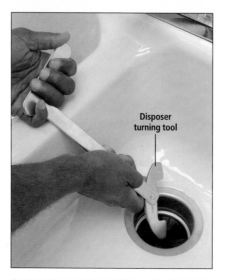

Disposer turning tool

Reset button

SOLVE JAMS WITH A SPECIAL TURNING TOOL.

Your disposer may come with an allen wrench that fits into a hole at the bottom of the disposer. If not, you can purchase a tool like the one shown. In either case, use the tool to turn the disposer back and forth. Once it rotates freely, make sure it is switched off, remove the obstruction, replace the splash guard, turn on the cold water, and test the disposer.

RESET AN OVERLOADED DISPOSER.

If your disposer motor shuts off during operation, its overload protector has sensed overheating and has broken the electrical connection. Wait a few minutes for the unit to cool, then push the red reset button on the bottom of the disposer. If that doesn't work, check the power to the unit: Inspect the cord and the fuse or circuit breaker.

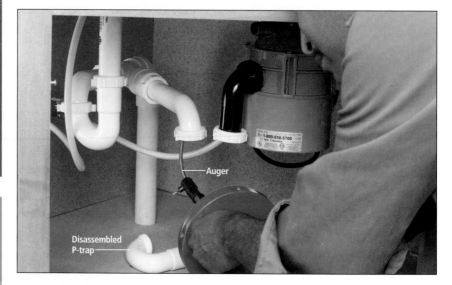

Auger

Disassembled P-trap

DISASSEMBLE AND AUGER THE DRAIN.

Because a disposer gobbles up huge amounts of food waste, you can expect the drain line to clog occasionally. If this happens, disassemble and remove the P-trap (make sure you have a bucket handy) and clean out the trap (see page 68). If the trap itself is clear, thread a drain auger into the drainpipe (see pages 69–70).

INSTALLING A DISHWASHER

Replacing an old dishwasher with a new one is a fairly simple job. Most units fit neatly into a 24-inch-wide undercounter cavity, and all are prewired and ready for simple supply, drain, and electrical hookups. Installing a new dishwasher, however, is a much larger job: You must make room for it and bring in electrical, supply, and drain lines. To avoid straining the discharge pump, position the dishwasher as near to the sink as possible.

YOU'LL NEED

TIME: About two hours to replace a dishwasher; a full day or more to install a new one.

SKILLS: Simple electrical and plumbing skills for replacing; carpentry and basic plumbing and electrical skills for a new installation.

TOOLS: Drill, electrical tools, carpentry tools, screwdriver, groove-joint pliers.

1 PREPARE THE OPENING.

Shut off the water and shut off the electrical power.

If you are replacing an existing dishwasher, remove its lower panel and disconnect the supply line, the drain hose, and the electrical line. Remove screws that attach it to the countertop and carefully pull out the unit.

For a new installation, remove a 24-inch-wide base cabinet or build a space to fit the dishwasher. Bore a hole large enough to allow for the supply and drain lines near the lower back of the side panel of the adjoining cabinet. The dishwasher will need its own 15- or 20-amp circuit. Run a circuit from the service panel (you may want to hire a licensed electrician to install this).

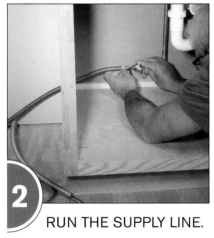

2 RUN THE SUPPLY LINE.

Cut into the hot water supply line and insert a standard tee fitting, a nipple, and a shutoff valve. Run flexible copper tubing into the cavity, leaving enough line to reach the dishwasher supply fitting. (See pages 142–155 for information on working with various types of pipes.)

3 PROVIDE A DRAIN FITTING.

You can drain the dishwasher either into the sink drain or into a garbage disposer, if you have one.

For sink drainage, install a dishwasher tailpiece. Loosen the slip nuts and remove the tailpiece, insert the dishwasher tailpiece into the trap, and cut the old tailpiece to fit above it. Connect all the pieces and tighten the slip nuts.

To drain a dishwasher into a garbage disposer, use a screwdriver and hammer to remove the metal knockout inside the drain nipple located near the top of the disposer. The knockout, when freed, may fall into the grinding chamber of the disposer—be sure to take it out.

Installing a dishwasher *(continued)*

4 ATTACH THE DRAIN LINE.

Thread the drain line through the hole in the cabinet and slip it onto the dishwasher tailpiece or drain nipple—you may have to push hard. Secure it with an automotive hose clamp.

To ensure proper operation of the appliance, the drain line must make a loop, so that at some point it is raised near the height of the countertop. The drain line will vibrate during use, so wrap a couple of lengths of wire around it and fasten them to screws driven into the underside of the countertop. Take care that the screws do not poke through the countertop.

Some local codes require an air gap at the top of the loop. You can place this in a knockout hole in the sink or drill a hole for it in the countertop. Run one line from the drain nipple to the air gap, another from the air gap to the dishwasher drain outlet.

5 MAKE THE HOOKUPS.

Position the ends of the water supply line, drain line, and electrical cable approximately at the locations where they will connect to the dishwasher. Remove the bottom coverplate from the dishwasher and slide the unit carefully into place, watching to make sure the lines are not damaged. Make sure the dishwasher is all the way in position.

Make the connections. Tighten the compression nut and drain line clamp firmly and make secure electrical connections.

Turn the leg's leveling screws to level the dishwasher. Anchor the dishwasher to the underside of the countertop with screws. Turn on the water and the electrical power. Before reattaching access panels, run the washer and watch for leaks.

This appliance gives you an immediate source of piping hot water for instant soup, tea, and coffee, as well as for quick blanching of vegetables.

Installation is relatively simple. The most difficult step is adding an electrical receptacle under the sink. You typically can't use the garbage disposer's receptacle because it works on a switch, and this one must be live all the time.

When you open the faucet valve, unheated water enters the dispenser through the supply tube, warming as it passes through the expansion chamber. The pressure of the incoming water forces hot water from the holding tank and expansion chamber (where it cools to 200°F) out the spout. When the temperature in the tank drops, a thermostat activates heating elements to return the water to the set temperature.

YOU'LL NEED

TIME: About three hours, not including installation of an electrical receptacle.

SKILLS: Drilling a clean hole, careful handling of flexible line, electrical skills.

TOOLS: Drill, holesaw or metal-boring holesaw, screwdriver, groove-joint pliers, wire strippers.

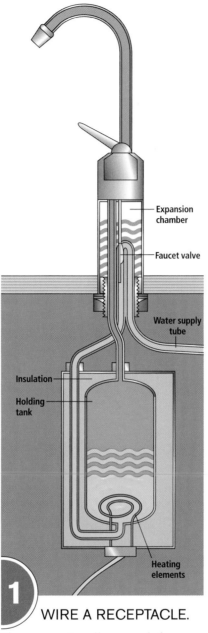

- Expansion chamber
- Faucet valve
- Water supply tube
- Insulation
- Holding tank
- Heating elements

1 WIRE A RECEPTACLE.

If necessary, install a grounded electrical receptacle that is always live under the sink, near the location of the dispenser. If your dispenser has a plug, codes require a GFCI receptacle within 6 feet of a water source. (See page 120 for installing the receptacle box.)

CAUTION

CHECK THE CIRCUIT

Any heating element draws a lot of current. If a circuit is already overloaded, you need to have an electrician install a grounded circuit of this unit. If your unit has a plug, be sure to install a ground fault circuit interrupter (GFCI) receptacle as well.

2 DRILL A HOLE.

Decide where you want to place the dispenser. If you have a stainless-steel sink, you can buy a holesaw designed to cut through metal. Drill slowly. (If you are installing a new sink, select one with an extra hole.)

Your sink may have a knockout hole. If it's the right size, just punch the insert out from below.

It may be easier to drill a hole near the back edge of the countertop near the sink, using a fine-tooth holesaw. Make sure you leave room for the entire diameter of the unit. Position the hole so the faucet is close enough to run into the sink.

Installing hot water dispensers *(continued)*

3 ATTACH THE FAUCET ASSEMBLY.

Insert the assembly with its gasket into the hole. You may need a helper to hold the dispenser in the correct position as you crawl underneath and work. Slip on the washer, screw on the mounting nut, and tighten firmly.

Tank mounting bracket

4 MOUNT THE TANK.

Place the tank mounting bracket 12 to 14 inches below the underside of the countertop, and make sure it's plumb before fastening it with screws. Mount the tank onto the bracket.

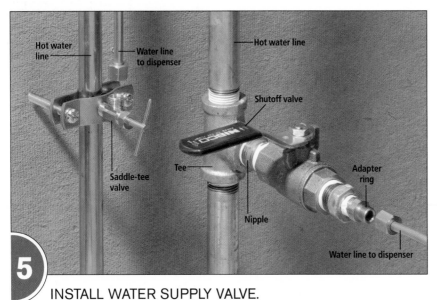

Hot water line — Water line to dispenser — Hot water line — Shutoff valve — Tee — Saddle-tee valve — Nipple — Adapter ring — Water line to dispenser

5 INSTALL WATER SUPPLY VALVE.

Shut off the water and drain the line. To supply the unit with water, tap into the hot water line that serves the sink. If codes permit, use a saddle-tee valve. Don't use the puncture-type saddle tee. Although it is easier to install, it clogs easily. Instead drill a small hole in the supply line, then secure the clamp to the line, as shown. If saddle tees are forbidden in your locality, you'll have some plumbing to do. Break into the line (see pages 92–93 and 142–149), and install a standard tee fitting. Add a nipple and a shutoff valve, as shown above right. Use an adapter fitting to make the transition to a flexible water line that matches your dispenser's supply line.

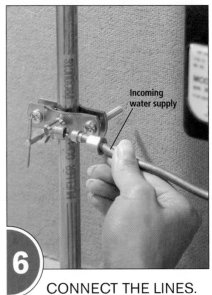

Incoming water supply

6 CONNECT THE LINES.

Secure the two longer tubes to the tank assembly and the shorter one to the water supply tube, using a compression nut and ferrule on each threaded fitting. The longer tubes are coded to prevent confusion. Restore water pressure and check for leaks. Let the tank fill before plugging in or turning on the unit.

INSTALLING A HOSE BIB

The task of replacing an existing hose bib faucet with a freeze-proof model or installing a new hose bib at a convenient location is at most a one-day job. Select a faucet that's long enough to reach well inside the heated house. Install it with a slight downward pitch toward the outside of the house so the pipe drains after closing the valve.

Even a freeze-proof faucet will freeze and rupture if a hose is left attached. An outdoor faucet remains the most vulnerable element to freezing in your plumbing system. Remove hoses before first frost. As the temperature falls below 32°F, the water in an exposed pipe freezes, expands, and ruptures the pipe. Ask any homeowner who has had to deal with one: A burst water pipe creates a costly mess.

This project assumes your house is plumbed with copper pipe. If you have galvanized steel pipes, install a dielectric union if you plan to connect copper pipe to the system.

1 DRAIN AND CUT THE SUPPLY PIPE.

Drill a hole through the house using a keyhole saw. The hole will need to be large enough for the hose bib shaft. From the outside, insert the shaft. Inside the house, locate and mark where you will be tapping into the existing supply line.

Turn off the main water supply valve nearest to the installation or replacement faucet. Drain the line at the main supply valve or a faucet lower than the elevation of the new faucet. The supply line must be completely drained of water and dry before you solder new copper connections. Remove aerators on faucets along the drained line.

Cut the copper pipe at the mark with a mini hacksaw or tubing cutter. Remove any burrs and clean the pipe.

2 SOLDER THE SUPPLY PIPE.

Solder a copper tee and any pipe necessary to install the hose bib stub (see pages 142–145). Solder a threaded adapter fitting to the copper pipe.

CAUTION

WATCH THAT FLAME

This job requires soldering with a propane torch. Wear eye protection and protect combustible materials with fire-resistant cloth or sheet metal. As a precaution, keep a fire extinguisher nearby.

3 INSTALL THE FAUCET.

Install a union between the adapter and the hose bib shaft. A union makes it easier to remove and replace the hose bib if it becomes damaged. It also means you don't have to turn the hose bib with a wrench to install it, which could damage it. Wrap all threaded fittings with plumber's tape (see page 151).

On the outside, drive screws through the mounting holes to secure the flange. Caulk around the flange to prevent cold air or unwanted pests from entering the house. Close the hose bib faucet valve. Close the drain cap, if open. Turn on the main supply and inspect for leaks. If you have removed faucet aerators, replace them after you flush the lines.

BEAUTY BEHIND THE WALLS Much of what makes for a beautiful shower is actually behind the walls. Beginning on page 132 you'll find the information you need to select and work with the pipes and fittings that are the bones of any plumbing project.

Tools
AND MATERIALS

One thing to remember when starting any project is that no matter how complex it may seem, it can be broken down to smaller, simpler projects and then reduced further to the tools and materials. Understanding the tools and materials determines the success or failure of every project.

This chapter identifies the different tools required for most plumbing projects. Learn which are essential tools and which are specialized tools. Some tools you may already have. Others you may want to purchase. Specialty tools tend to be job specific and expensive, so you may want to rent them from a local rental store rather than purchase. A discussion of organizing your tools presents ideas on how to avoid clutter so that you can find the right tool when you need it, saving time and frustration.

Knowing how to choose the right materials is essential for any plumbing project. You will learn how to select the right pipe and fittings, how to measure pipes and fittings, and how to map your home plumbing system. Equipped with this knowledge, you can confidently begin any plumbing project.

IT STARTS WITH THE TOOLS
You'll need the right tools and materials to achieve a master bath such as this one that's worthy of a relaxing soak. Beginning on page 130 are suggestions for assembling the tools necessary to complete the projects in this book.

ESSENTIAL TOOLS

Plumbing does not require a lot of expensive tools, and some that you may use for only one job are well worth the cost. The money you save by doing your own work pays for them many times over. Using the tools shown on this page, you can tackle most plumbing projects.

To clear drain lines, get a plunger. The type shown here, with the extra flange extending downward, is ideal for toilets and also works well on bathtubs and sinks. Use a hand-cranked drain auger to clear away clogs that resist simple plunging. For toilets, use a closet auger.

To disassemble and connect pipes and to make myriad plumbing repairs, purchase a pair of groove-joint pliers, which adjust to grab various size pipes. A standard adjustable pipe wrench is essential for working with threaded iron pipe. An adjustable wrench fits the nuts on faucets and other fixtures. All come in various sizes, each fitting a minimum and maximum size pipe.

To cut pipe, use a hacksaw. Hacksaw blades dull quickly, so have extra blades available.

For running new pipes through walls, you will need a drill with plenty of spade bits. To cut away drywall or plaster to make room for the plumbing, use a keyhole saw. A flashlight comes in handy when you need to peer into wall cavities and under sinks.

For delicate chores such as removing faucet O-rings and clips, have a pair of needle-nose pliers on hand. And have a ready supply of general purpose tools, including screwdrivers, a putty knife, a utility knife, and a tape measure.

Auger

Drill

Flashlight

Plunger

Spade bits

Screwdrivers

Closet auger

Hacksaw

Keyhole saw

Pipe wrench

Needle-nose pliers

Tape measure

Adjustable wrench

Groove-joint pliers

Putty knife

Utility knife

SPECIALIZED TOOLS

ome tools are designed for specialized plumbing tasks. Choose the ones that will most help you work with your materials and fixtures.

If you need to solder copper pipe, you must have a propane torch. If you have a lot to do, pay the extra money for a self-igniting model. Otherwise get an inexpensive spark lighter.

To bend flexible copper tubing without kinking it, use a tubing bender. A two-part flaring tool is necessary if you want to make flare joints in copper tubing. If you plan on

cutting copper pipe or tubing, buy a tubing cutter. It makes easier and cleaner cuts than a hacksaw and will not squeeze tubing out of shape. For cutting plastic supply pipes, a plastic tubing cutter makes the job easier. To set the proper incline for drain pipes, you'll need a level.

When working on faucets and sinks, you will sometimes need a basin wrench to get at nuts you can't reach with pliers. If you have a damaged faucet seat that needs replacing, don't take a chance with a screwdriver—use a seat wrench. For

those big nuts that secure the basket strainers of kitchen sinks, you may need a spud wrench.

When plunging and augering fail to clear out a clog, a blow bag might do the trick: Hook up a garden hose to it, insert it into the drainpipe, and turn on the water.

For large-scale demolition, notching studs and joists, and quickly cutting galvanized pipe, a reciprocating saw is indispensable. If you need to chip away tiles to get at plumbing, use a cold chisel.

Spark lighter

Blow bag

Propane torch

Basin wrench

Reciprocating saw

Flaring tool

Plastic tubing cutter

Spud wrench

Hacksaw

Tubing cutter

Cold chisel

Seat wrench

Tubing bender

Level

CHOOSING PIPE

First you must determine what kind of pipe you have in your home. It's often easiest to use the same type when adding on, but you don't have to. To change type, you must purchase special adapter fittings that connect one material to another in the middle of a pipe run.

Supply lines—the pipes that carry pressurized water to your fixtures—usually are copper and plastic. However, if your home is old enough to have galvanized pipe and you need to install only a short run of pipe, it makes sense to continue with galvanized piping. In many localities, plastic supply pipe is not allowed. Keep in mind that you'll have to learn how to solder in order to use copper pipe (see pages 142–145).

To make final connections to a fixture or a faucet, install a flexible supply line. Use copper (see page 146) or plastic flexible tubing, and be careful to avoid kinks.

Plastic pipe—either PVC (polyvinyl-chloride) or ABS (acrylonitrile-butadiene-styrene)—is now used almost exclusively for drains. If you have old cast-iron, galvanized, or copper drainpipes, make

CPVC

PVC

ABS

Black steel

Galvanized steel

Flexible copper

Rigid copper

Cast iron

Flexible PE

Flexible PB

the transition to plastic. It is much easier to install and less expensive.

Before you buy any pipe, check with the local building department to make sure you're using material approved for use in your area.

GAS LINES

Gas lines are almost always made of black steel pipe. It has the same texture as galvanized pipe but not the shiny silver color. You install black steel pipe the same way you install galvanized pipe (see page 151). Check for leaks by turning the gas on, brushing soapy water on the joints, and looking for tiny bubbles.

Depending on local building codes, you may be allowed to use galvanized pipe for gas, but it's more expensive. Do not use copper pipe for long gas lines. A chemical reaction causes the inside of the pipe to flake, and a buildup of flakes damages appliances.

COMMON PIPE SIZES

Nominal pipe sizes commonly used in residential plumbing in North America.
(See pages 136–137)

- The main water supply line that enters a house is ¾ or 1 inch.

- Water supply lines after the water heater usually are ½-inch pipe, sometimes ¾-inch pipe.

- Gas lines are most often ¾-inch and sometimes ½-inch pipe.

- Main drainpipes, called stacks, are 3 or 4 inches in diameter.

- Kitchen, tub, and shower drains are almost always 1½-inch pipes.

- Bathroom sink drains are almost always 1¼-inch pipes.

CHOOSING PIPE

Material	Type	Uses (check local codes)	Features and Joining Techniques
Copper	Rigid	Hot and cold supply lines; rarely for DWV (drain-waste-vent) lines	Sold in 10' and 20' lengths. The most widely used pipe for supply lines. Lightweight and durable, though a bit expensive. Once you learn the soldering technique, it goes together quickly. Type M is the thinnest and is a good choice for home projects. Types L and K are used mainly in commercial projects.
	Flexible	Hot and cold supply lines, for short final runs to fixtures	Comes in easy-to-bend 60' and 100' coils, or by the foot. Can be soldered like rigid copper but usually is connected with compression fittings.
Threaded steel	Galvanized	Supply and occasionally DWV	Because it's cumbersome to work with and tends to build up lime deposits that constrict water flow, it is not used widely anymore. Expensive equipment is required to cut and thread it, so users must buy precut pieces from suppliers. If you have a good selection of shorter pieces on hand, you can cut down on trips to the supplier.
	Black	Gas line	Rusts readily, so it can't be used for water supply.
Plastic	ABS	DWV only	Black in color, in 10' or 20' lengths. Lightweight and easy to work with, it cuts with an ordinary saw and cements together with a special glue. Check local codes before using.
	PVC	Cold water supply and DWV	Cream-colored, blue-gray, or white, PVC comes in 10' or 20' lengths. This has the same properties as ABS, except that you must apply primer before cementing it. Do not mix PVC with ABS or interchange their cements.
	CPVC	Hot and cold supply lines	White, gray, or cream-colored, CPVC is available in 10' lengths. Has the same properties as ABS and PVC.
	Flexible PB polybutylene	Hot and cold supply lines, usually for short runs	White or cream-colored, flexible PB is sold in 25' or 100' coils or by the foot. Expensive and not widely used, it is joined with special fittings.
	Flexible PE (polyethylene)	Supply lines	Black-colored, sold in 25' or 100' coils or by the foot. Same properties as PB. Used for sprinkler systems.
Cast-iron	Hub-and-Spigot	DWV	Extremely heavy and difficult to work with, so don't try to install new pipes of this material. Hub-and-spigot is joined with oakum and molten lead.
	No-Hub	DWV	Joins with gaskets and clamps, but still is hard to work with. Make the transition to plastic instead.

CHOOSING THE RIGHT FITTING

The parts bins at plumbing suppliers contain hundreds of fittings that give you the ability to connect almost any pipe materials. To get the best pipe for your needs, familiarize yourself with the terms on this page.

Supply fittings connect the pipes that bring water to fixtures and faucets. When changing direction in a supply run, use an elbow (ell). The most common ones make 90- or 45-degree turns and have female threads on each end. A street ell has male and female connections to allow for insertion into another fitting. A reducing ell joins one size pipe to another. Use a drop ell to anchor the pipes to framing where they will protrude into a room.

Use tees wherever two runs intersect. A reducing tee lets you join pipes of different diameters; for example, if you want to add a ½-inch branch to a ¾-inch main supply.

A coupling connects pipes end to end. Reducing couplings let you step down from one pipe diameter to a smaller one. Slip couplings (see page 153) function the same way unions do, joining sections of copper or plastic line. Use a cap to seal off a line.

A plastic-to-copper transition fitting is one of many transition fittings that connect one pipe material to another. (Do not make the transition from steel to copper without a special dielectric fitting, or the joint will corrode.)

In any run of threaded pipe, you'll need a union somewhere. This fitting compensates for the frustrating fact that you can't simultaneously turn a pipe into fittings at either end.

Nipples—lengths of pipe less than 12 inches long—are sold in standard sizes because short pieces are difficult to cut and thread.

Examine drainage fittings, and you'll see how they're designed to keep wastewater flowing downhill. Sometimes called sanitary fittings, they have gentle curves rather than sharp angles, so waste won't get hung up.

Choose ¼ bends to make 90-degree turns and ⅛ bends for 45 degrees. Also available are ⅕ bends for 72-degree turns and ⅙ bends for 60 degrees. All types of bends also come in more gradual curves, known as long-turn bends, which make for a smoother flow.

Sanitary branches, such as the tee and cross, come in a variety of configurations that suit situations where two or more lines converge. These can be tricky to order, so make a sketch of your proposed drain lines, identifying all pipe sizes, and take it to your supplier when you order.

Toilet hookups require a closet bend, which connects to the main drain, and a closet flange, which fits onto the bend. The flange is anchored to the floor and anchors the toilet bowl. To connect a sink trap to the drainpipe, use a trap adapter. To make the transition from cast-iron drain to plastic drain, use a no-hub adapter.

ORDERING OR FINDING FITTINGS

When ordering materials, organize your description of a fitting in this way: first the size, then the material, and finally the type of fitting. You might, for example, ask or look for a ½-inch galvanized, 90-degree ell. With reducing fittings, the larger size comes first, then the smaller.

Copper supply

Galvanized supply

Plastic supply

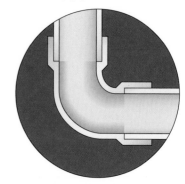

Plastic drain

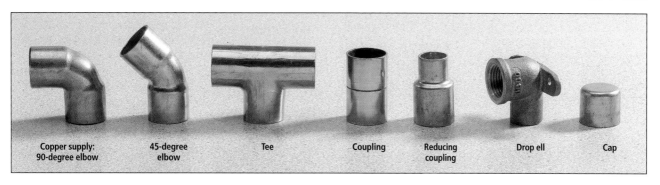

Copper supply: 90-degree elbow   45-degree elbow   Tee   Coupling   Reducing coupling   Drop ell   Cap

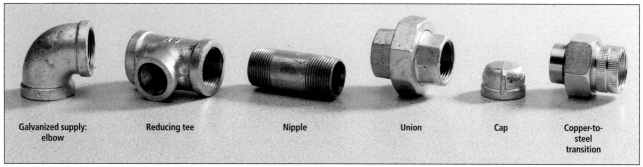

Galvanized supply: elbow   Reducing tee   Nipple   Union   Cap   Copper-to-steel transition

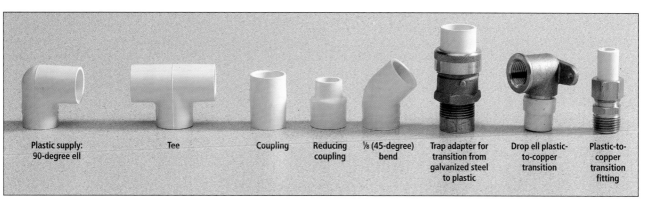

Plastic supply: 90-degree ell   Tee   Coupling   Reducing coupling   ⅛ (45-degree) bend   Trap adapter for transition from galvanized steel to plastic   Drop ell plastic-to-copper transition   Plastic-to-copper transition fitting

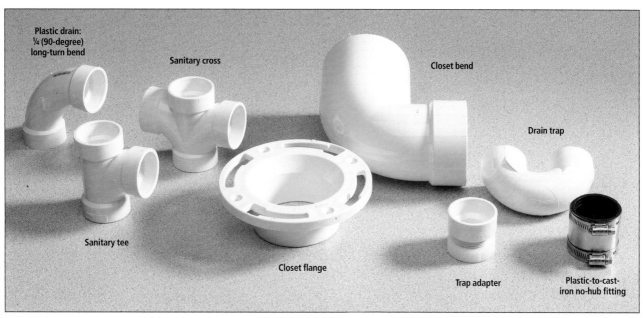

Plastic drain: ¼ (90-degree) long-turn bend   Sanitary cross   Closet bend   Drain trap   Sanitary tee   Closet flange   Trap adapter   Plastic-to-cast-iron no-hub fitting

MEASURING PIPES AND FITTINGS

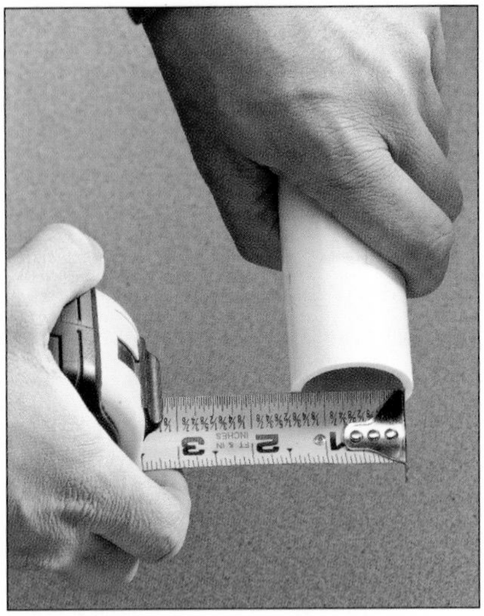

TO FIND OUT A PIPE'S SIZE, MEASURE THE INSIDE...

If you have a pipe with an exposed end, simply measure the pipe's inside diameter, and round off to the nearest ⅛ inch. Some manufacturers indicate the size on the fittings.

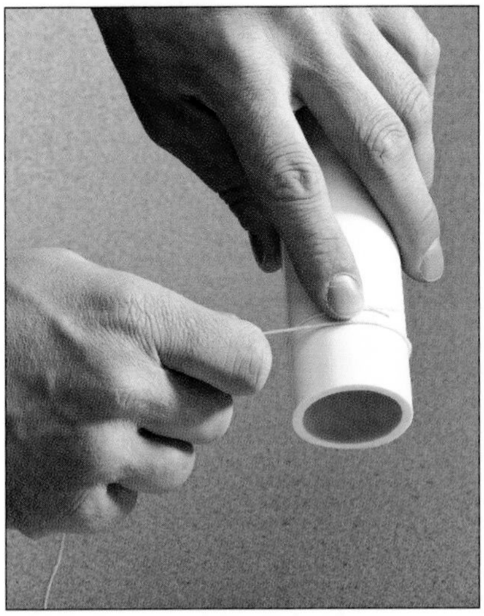

OR FIGURE FROM THE OUTSIDE.

You also can determine pipe size by measuring its outside circumference. Wrap a string around the pipe, straighten it out, and measure it. Use the chart below to find the nominal size you'll need to order.

It takes practice and experience to be able to figure out all the pipes and fittings you need before starting a job, so novice plumbers often spend more time running back and forth to their supplier than they do on the actual work. The first step in becoming an efficient plumber is to learn to correctly identify the pipes and fittings a job requires.

Plumbing dimensions aren't necessarily what they appear to be. A plastic pipe with a ⅞-inch outside diameter, for instance, is actually called a ½-inch pipe because it has a ½-inch inside diameter (ID). Pipes usually are sized according to their ID (see chart below). This dimension is also called the nominal size, the size you ask for at a plumbing supplier.

If you are at all unsure about getting the right material, specify the ID for most pipes. In a minority of cases—flexible copper lines, for

MEASUREMENTS: PIPE DIMENSIONS

Material	Inside Diameter (ID) Nominal Size	Approximate Outside Diameter (OD)	Approximate Circumference	Approximate Socket Depth
Copper	¼"	⅜"	1⅛"	5/16"
	⅜"	½"	1½"	⅜"
	½"	⅝"	2"	½"
	¾"	⅞"	2¾"	¾"
	1"	1⅛"	3½"	15/16"
	1¼"	1⅜"	4 5/16"	1"
	1½"	1⅝"	5⅛"	1⅛"
Threaded steel	⅜"	⅝"	2"	⅜"
	½"	¾"	2⅜"	½"
	¾"	1"	3⅛"	9/16"
	1"	1¼"	4"	11/16"
	1¼"	1½"	4¾"	11/16"
	1½"	1¾"	5½"	11/16"
	2"	2¼"	7"	¾"
Plastic	½"	⅞"	2¾"	½"
	¾"	1⅛"	3½"	⅝"
	1"	1⅜"	4 5/16"	¾"
	1¼"	1⅝"	5⅛"	11/16"
	1½"	1⅞"	6"	11/16"
	2"	2⅜"	7½"	¾"
	3"	3⅜"	10½"	1½"
	4"	4⅜"	14"	1¾"
Cast-iron	2"	2¼"	7"	2½"
	3"	3¼"	10⅛"	2¾"
	4"	4¼"	13⅜"	3"

example—pipe is ordered using the outside diameter (OD).

If you can measure the inside dimension, you're job is easier. However, often you won't have a way of measuring the inside of the pipe. Holding a ruler against a pipe will give you only a rough idea of the outside diameter. Instead, use a string or a set of calipers for a more exact measurement. Once you find the outside dimension, use the chart, opposite, to find the nominal size.

Fittings can be just as confusing. Their inside diameters must be large enough to fit over the pipe's outside diameter. A ½-inch plastic elbow, for example, has an outside diameter of about 1¼ inches.

As a rule of thumb, copper pipe's OD is ⅛ inch greater than its ID, the nominal size. For plastic pipe, measure the OD and subtract ⅜ inch. For threaded and cast-iron, subtract ¼ inch.

Another mathematical pitfall for a novice plumber is measuring the length of a pipe that runs from one fitting to the next. Pipes must fully extend into fixture and fitting sockets (see illustrations, right), or the joint could leak. Socket depths vary from one pipe size and material to another, so you must account for the depth of each fitting's socket in the total length of pipe needed between fittings.

The only times you don't have to take socket depth into account are when you are using no-hub cast-iron pipes (see page 95) or slip couplings with copper or plastic pipe.

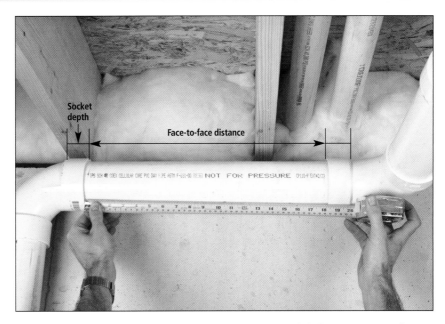

Fully joined pipe

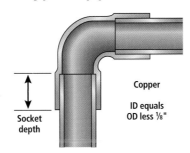

Copper
ID equals OD less ⅛"

Socket depth

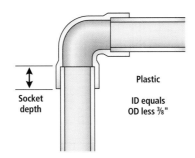

Plastic
ID equals OD less ⅜"

Socket depth

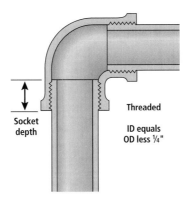

Threaded
ID equals OD less ¼"

Socket depth

ADD THE SOCKET DEPTHS.

To determine the length of a pipe, first measure from face to face, as shown above. Then check the chart on page 136 for the socket depth of the material you're working with. Because pipes have fittings on both ends, multiply by 2, and add the face-to-face length.

MEASURE COPPER OR PLASTIC IN PLACE.

When working with copper or plastic—materials you can cut on the job—often the most accurate way of measuring is to insert the pipe into one fitting and mark the other end, rather than using a tape measure.

GET MULTIPLE CAPS

Don't leave the household high and dry while you drive back and forth to the plumbing supplier. When buying fittings, invest in a handful of caps in different sizes. That way, if you've misread a dimension—as even experienced plumbers do occasionally—you can easily cap off the line and turn the water on again.

The plumbing in households remains hidden, for the most part, behind floors, walls, and cabinets. If you venture into the unfinished portion of the basement or the part of the house that contains the heating system and water heater, you'll possibly see runs of copper water supply pipe or a drain stack made of PVC or cast-iron. You may have even seen the small vent stacks of the drain-waste-vent system on the roof. Most people don't notice the plumbing system, except when there's a problem. Then it becomes a mysterious nuisance.

Before attempting a project, know and understand your plumbing system. If you are fortunate to have a blueprint of the plumbing drawings of your house, you can easily follow, understand, and know the location of piping, venting, and fixtures in your home. Though some plumbers stray from their plans slightly, the blueprint should be accurate. Make additional copies and mark the corrections as you find them on the copy. Also use the copies to plan and record modifications and additions to the plumbing system. If you don't have a blueprint of the plumbing system, grab graph paper, clipboard, a scale, straightedge, and pencil to create your own.

RECORD THE LOCATION OF HOUSE PLUMBING.

Having an accurate drawing will make responding to an emergency easier, as well as simplify remodeling of or additions to the system. To follow the route of a pipe, start where the main supply line enters the home. Continue to map the pipe to where it connects to the water heater. At that point, the pipe will exit the water heater with a hot and cold line. Mark the locations where these pipes branch off toward fixtures throughout the house. Remember that supply pipes must end near a drainpipe. When mapping the drainpipe system, work backwards for the fixtures, mapping as you go.

You may find an access panel behind a bathtub or shower. Removing the panel reveals the plumbing. Note from which directions the supply pipes enter the wall. Record the locations of any valves you come across.

Some older homes have hot water heat supplied from a boiler. Map these lines separately.

Mapping symbols

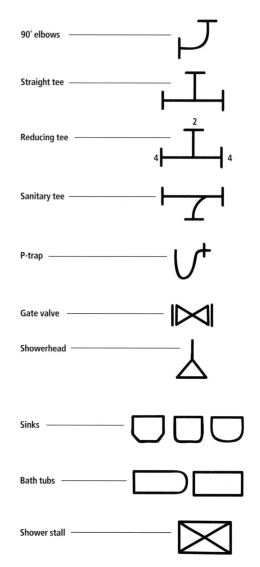

90° elbows

Straight tee

Reducing tee

Sanitary tee

P-trap

Gate valve

Showerhead

Sinks

Bath tubs

Shower stall

LOCATE THE WATER METER.

Know the location of the water meter. You'll find the main shutoff valve for the house adjacent to it. Some homes have shutoff valves on both sides of the meter. If you don't see a shutoff valve near the water meter, follow the line to where it enters your house. There should be a shutoff valve located along it. In warm

climates, the shutoff valve might be located on the outside of the home, sometimes in a plastic or concrete box called a buffalo box. Homes built in colder regions may have the main shutoff valve buried below the frost line. A "key" is used to reach the valve through a valve box above the valve. If you still can't locate the shutoff, contact your local municipal water supplier. Once you locate the meter and shutoff valve, measure and mark both locations using the proper plumbing symbols.

MEASURE AND RECORD ALL PIPE RUNS.

Mark the location of supply and wastewater pipes as they run horizontally along floor joists and vertically (called a riser) into the floor above. As you follow a horizontally run pipe, remember that it's not unusual for pipe to change from horizontal to vertical and back again.

IDENTIFY ALL CLEANOUT HUBS.

Older homes have main stacks of cast-iron construction; newer home construction uses plastic pipe for the stacks and drain/waste system. Stacks usually run straight through the roof. You'll find a cleanout hub near the lowest point of the stack. You may also find cleanouts along the drainpipe runs. Include all cleanouts on your map. Note the location of each with measurements. Should the pipes have a backup or blockage, these locations will make clearing out the blockage easier.

RECORD SHUTOFF VALVE LOCATIONS.

Seek out the locations of all shutoff valves in your home. Record them on your map. In an emergency such as a burst pipe, you will be able to quickly find the valve and shut off the water.

FINDING HIDDEN PIPES

Follow these steps to find pipes that run behind walls or through enclosed floors and ceilings:

■ Determine which valves control which fixtures by closing the valves. Check which fixtures do not have water.

■ Most basic interior walls are approximately 4 inches thick. If you find a wall that is thicker, it probably contains a main vent stack.

■ Locating secondary stacks can be difficult. Have a helper feed an auger down the roof vent while you locate the sound from inside.

■ Use the unique sounds pipe make to assist in identifying them. Drainpipes make a gurgling sound and supply pipes have more of a hissing sound. An old plumber's trick to locate and determine which is which is to place the open end of a drinking glass against the wall. Put your ear on the bottom of the glass. The glass magnifies sound.

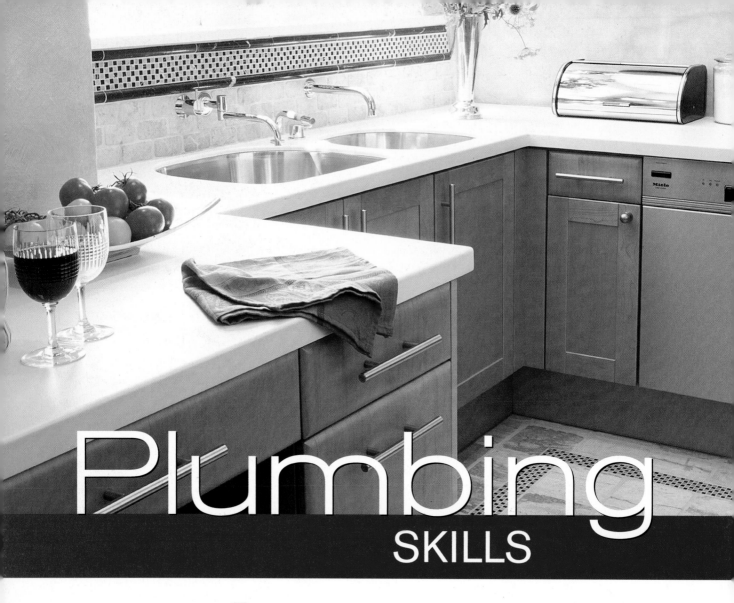

Plumbing
SKILLS

The unknown is almost always intimidating. When faced with something new—such as plumbing—you no doubt will question your abilities. Where to start? What to do? Should you call in an expert or try to fix it yourself? The best time to ask yourself those questions is not when you're standing beneath a pipe that is showering you and turning the basement into an indoor pool.

Plumbing is all about technique and understanding basic physics. Mastering any technique requires practice. Before diving into any of the projects included in this book, practice the skills you will need. Don't expect to barge through a project without the proper techniques—especially if they are new to you—and expect perfect results.

This section prepares you by giving examples of how to use the tools and materials required to complete the projects in this book. You'll begin by learning how to work with rigid copper pipe and flexible tubing. You'll learn how to install compression and flare fittings. You'll understand how to work with threaded pipe. The last section explains how to work with different types of plastic pipe. Once you understand the techniques of plumbing, you're ready to begin.

READY, SET, UPGRADE

If you're ready to update your kitchen with new plumbing but are uncertain of where to begin, turn to page 142 to learn the basics of working with pipes and fittings. These fundamental plumbing skills will allow you to complete most home plumbing jobs.

PICTURE-PERFECT PLUMBING

Before you start removing old fixtures, sinks, and toilets to renovate an outdated, leaky bathroom, brush up on the skills necessary to do the job right. This chapter covers the behind-the-scenes techniques to update or create a room worthy of a photo.

WORKING WITH RIGID COPPER PIPE

Soldering rigid copper plumbing is a skill unique to plumbing work. Learning takes some time, but once you get the knack, soldering is quicker than screwing together threaded pipe.

Sometimes soldering is called "sweating." It relies on capillary action to flow molten solder into the fitting. Just as an ink blotter soaks up ink, a joint absorbs molten solder, making a watertight bond that's as strong as the pipe itself. Any gaps will leak. Be sure that the joint has an even bead of solder around its circumference to prevent leaks.

ELIMINATING MOISTURE

If you are adding on to existing plumbing, you may find a little water inside the pipes. You must dry pipes completely before soldering. If possible, tilt the pipes to allow water to flow out. Heat the area of existing pipe to evaporate any water; open faucets on the line to allow steam to escape.

Stuff in a piece of white bread (not the crust) just upstream of the connection. It will absorb the water and dissolve when the water is turned on. You can also buy specially made capsules that plug the line while you work. When the work is finished, heat from a torch melts the capsule away.

YOU'LL NEED

TIME: With practice, an hour to connect five joints.

SKILLS: Soldering is a specialized skill that takes time to learn.

TOOLS: Tubing cutter or hacksaw, emery cloth, wire brush, flux brush, propane torch, groove-joint pliers.

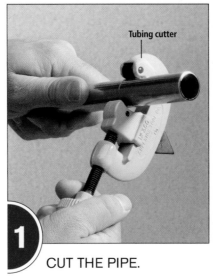

1 CUT THE PIPE.

Use a tubing cutter or a hacksaw. A tubing cutter makes cleaner cuts. Clamp the cutter onto the tubing, rotate a few revolutions, tighten, and rotate some more. Make hacksaw cuts in a miter box. Don't nick the metal—this could cause the connection to leak.

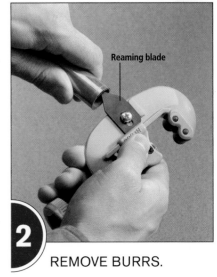

2 REMOVE BURRS.

Remove burrs on the inside of the pipe by inserting the reaming blade of the tubing cutter and twisting. If you don't have a tubing cutter, use a metal file.

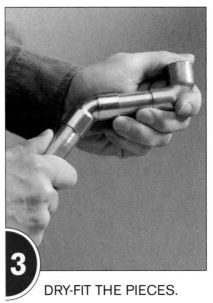

3 DRY-FIT THE PIECES.

Dry-fit a number of pipe pieces and fittings to make sure they are the right length. If you have difficulty pushing pieces together because the pipe was squeezed out of shape during cutting, cut a new piece. Most pros lay out an entire run of copper, cutting and dry-fitting all of its components. Once you are satisfied, take the pipes apart and set them on a clean surface.

4 POLISH THE PIPE AND FITTING.

Polish the outside of the pipe and the inside of the fitting with emery cloth or steel wool. Doing so removes grease, dirt, and oxidation that could impede the flow of solder. Stop polishing when the metal is shiny. Avoid touching polished surfaces—oil from your fingers will interfere with the solder flow and cause a leak.

5 APPLY FLUX.

Brush a light, even coating of flux (also called soldering paste) onto both surfaces. Flux retards oxidation when the copper is heated. As solder flows into the joint, the flux burns away. Use a resin- (not acid-) type flux for plumbing work.

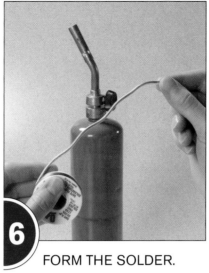

6 FORM THE SOLDER.

Bend the solder so it's easy to work with but long enough to keep your fingers away from the flame. Unwind about 10 inches of solder, straighten it, and bend 2 inches at a 60-degree angle. Light the torch. Adjust the flame until the inner (blue) cone is about 2 inches long.

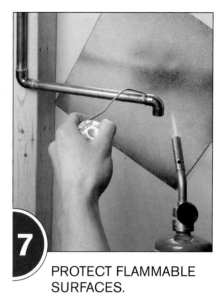

7 PROTECT FLAMMABLE SURFACES.

If you're working near framing, paper-sheathed insulation, or other flammable materials, shield them from the propane torch flame with an old cookie sheet or a piece of sheet metal.

Heat the fitting, not the joint.

8 ASSEMBLE THE CONNECTION.

Heat the middle of the fitting—not the joint—with the inner cone of the flame. Touch the solder to the joint. If it is hot enough, capillary action will pull solder into the joint. Remove the flame when solder drips from the pipe.

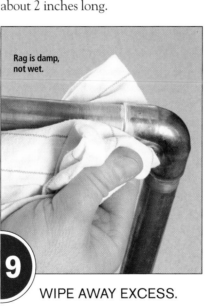

Rag is damp, not wet.

9 WIPE AWAY EXCESS.

For a neat, professional look, lightly brush the joint with a damp rag. Take care not to burn your fingers.

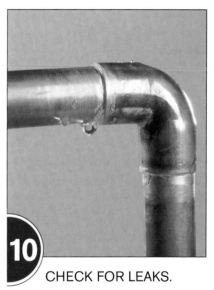

10 CHECK FOR LEAKS.

Turn on the water to test the system. If you have a leak, there is no easy solution—you can't fix a leak while water is present. Shut off the water, drain the line, disassemble the joint (see page 144), and discard the old fitting. Dry the inside of the pipes. Polish the pipe end and the inside of the new fitting, apply flux, reassemble, and solder again.

Working with rigid copper pipe *(continued)*

Installing a brass valve

11 INSTALL PIPE HANGERS.

Copper supply lines need support at least every 6 feet. The plastic type of hanger pictured here is easy to install, helps quiet noisy pipes, and is slightly flexible so it doesn't damage the pipes.

Brass valve

1 REMOVE HEAT-SENSITIVE PARTS.

A valve stem has rubber or plastic parts that will melt during soldering. Remove the stem with a wrench. Polish the pipe end and the inside of the fitting as you would a copper joint.

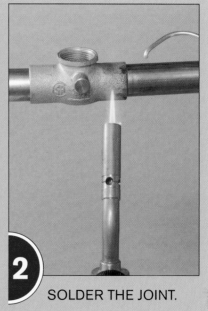

2 SOLDER THE JOINT.

Fit the pieces together. (If the valve has an arrow, be sure it points in the direction of water flow.) Heat the body of the valve, moving the flame back and forth to heat both sides evenly. Brass requires more heating than copper. Apply solder as you would with a copper fitting.

Taking apart soldered joints

1 HEAT THE FITTING.

Shut off the water and drain the line. Light a propane torch, set it so the inner (blue) cone of the flame is about 2 inches long, and heat the fitting. Point the flame at both sides of the fitting, not directly at the soldered joint.

2 PULL THE PIECES APART.

Once the fitting is heated, you have only a few seconds to take the joint apart. Prepare a safe place to set the torch and have two pairs of pliers within easy reach. Work carefully—the pipes are very hot. While the pipe is hot, grasp the fitting and pipe with pliers and pull the joint apart.

3 POLISH THE PIPE ENDS.

To remove old solder, heat the pipe end with the torch and quickly wipe with a dry rag. Do this carefully—the pipe is very hot. Allow the pipe to cool and polish the end with emery cloth. Never reuse old copper fittings—only a new fitting can create a watertight seal.

Using a propane torch

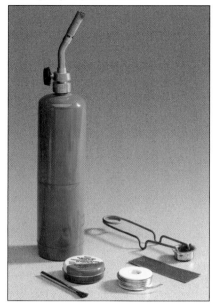

INSPECT THE EQUIPMENT.

Gases are produced when using a propane torch. Carbon monoxide is the most dangerous byproduct. It is odorless, colorless, and toxic in a confined space. Open a window and position a small fan to remove fumes.

Read the instructions provided by the manufacturer of the propane torch. Pay special attention to the cylinder seals and torch nozzles. If you see any damage, return the torch to the store and exchange it for a new one.

To light the torch, first open the valve and then strike a spark. You can use a spark lighter. If you don't have a spark lighter, a match also works. Adjust the valve until the blue flame is 1 to 2 inches long.

Always close the torch valve when you are finished with it. Hand-tighten the seal, but be careful not to over-tighten it.

SOLDERING SAFELY.

Running a new copper supply line requires negotiating turns and working in tight places. You may find yourself having to solder fittings inside confining access panels and between floor joists. Inspect each area. A propane torch produces a flame. Look for potential fire hazards. Isolate them or place a protective barrier between the joint to be soldered and the flammable object.

You can purchase a flameproof barrier at your local home center or hardware store. The barriers are constructed o f a flame-retardant material. Some manufacturers put grommets in the corners to allow you to hang or nail them in place, thus freeing your hands. An old cookie sheet also works as an excellent barrier. As an added safety measure, always keep a fire extinguisher handy while working.

SOLDERING SAFETY TIPS

Soldering presents a triple safety risk. The lead solder, the fumes, and the solder and propane torch are hot enough to instantly burn flesh. Use the following rules for safe soldering.

- Wear eye protection, either a face shield or safety glasses. Eyes may become irritated when exposed to the smoke. Avoid wearing contact lenses as the fumes can get under the lenses and cause severe irritation.

- When cutting off leads, make sure they do not fly away.

- Avoid breathing smoke/fumes produced during soldering. Use a small fan to remove the fumes. Inhaling flux fumes during soldering may cause irritation and damage of mucous membranes and respiratory system.

- When ventilating the room is not sufficient, an approved respirator should be worn.

- Legs and arms should be covered to avoid burns from splashed hot solder.

- Wash your hands thoroughly after handling solder. Use only lead-free solder.

WORKING WITH FLEXIBLE COPPER TUBING

Flexible copper tubing is pliable enough to make all but the sharpest turns. When you use it, you don't have to install a fitting every time you make a turn as you would with rigid pipe. In almost every case, you will connect flexible tubing to compression and flare fittings (see pages 147–149) instead of soldering them.

Do not use copper tubing for a gas line. Natural gas will cause the inside of the copper tube to flake, which can damage appliances.

YOU'LL NEED

TIME: About 15 minutes to bend and cut tubing for a short run.

SKILLS: Handling and cutting copper tubing.

TOOLS: Tubing cutter, coil-spring tubing bender.

1 UNCOIL THE TUBING.

Because flexible copper tubing is soft, always handle it gently. As you uncoil tubing, straighten it out every few inches as you go. If the tubing comes in a box, grip the box and carefully pull the tubing upward.

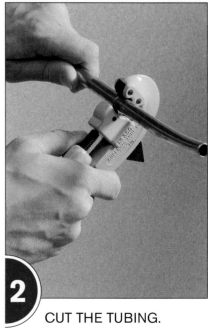

2 CUT THE TUBING.

Cut flexible tubing with a tubing cutter or a hacksaw. Insert and twist the reaming blade of the tubing cutter to remove burrs on the inside of the tubing. Or use a metal file.

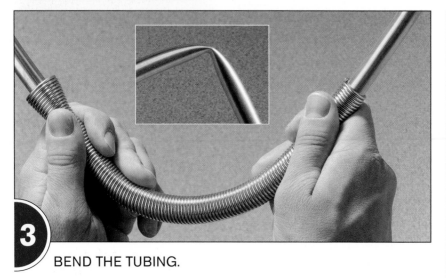

3 BEND THE TUBING.

Bend the flexible tubing in gradual, sweeping arcs. If you don't, it will surprise you by suddenly kinking, and you'll have to throw the piece away. Kinks seriously impede water flow and are almost impossible to reshape.

If you need to make a fairly tight turn, use a coil-spring tubing bender like the one shown here. Slide the bender to the point you need a tight bend and, with it in place, bend the tubing. Then remove the bender. With one of these tools, it is nearly impossible to kink the tubing.

POLISH THE END

To complete your work with flexible copper tubing, rub the end of the tubing lightly with emery cloth to remove dirt and grease. With compression or flare fittings, you don't need to polish as much as you will for a soldered joint. To join tubing, solder the pieces together (see pages 142–145), or use compression fittings (see pages 147–148) or flare fittings (see page 149).

Use compression fittings in places where you may need to take the run apart someday or where it is difficult to solder. One common location is on supply lines for a sink, which have compression fittings at both the stop valve and the faucet inlet. Flexible supply lines are an even easier way to make this connection (see page 41).

Compression fittings usually are used with flexible copper tubing, but you can also use type-M rigid copper (see page 132–133). These fittings are not as strong as soldered joints, so they should not be hidden inside walls.

Use compression fittings to connect plastic supply tubing for refrigerator icemakers. The difference between a compression fitting designed for copper and one that is designed for plastic tubing is that the copper fitting will have a metal compression ring, while the plastic fitting will have a plastic compression ring. Using the wrong fitting on the wrong material will create leaks, so don't do it. Other than the one difference between the two fittings, installation is the same for both.

Never overtighten a fitting, especially when using plastic tubing. Once you encounter resistance when tightening, don't be tempted to give it an additional half turn. Test the integrity of the connection first. Slightly open the water supply valve. If it leaks, turn the water off and tighten a quarter turn. Retest the line. If it continues to leak, tighten quarter turn and test each time until the leak stops.

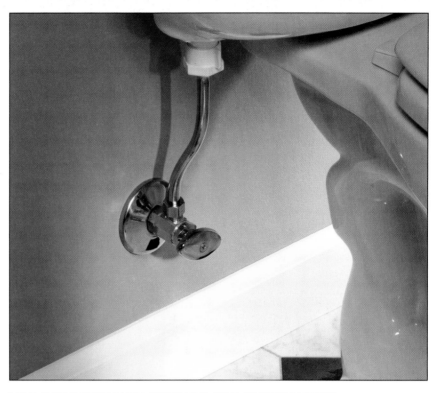

USE COMPRESSION FITTINGS FOR SUPPLY LINES.

Compression fittings are commonly used on fixtures where you may need to disconnect them in the future.

Common locations are on supply lines for sinks and toilets.

1 TO MAKE A COMPRESSION JOINT, POSITION THE PARTS.

Bend the tubing into position (see page 146), and slip on the nut and the ferrule. The ferrule will not go on if the tubing end is bent or isn't perfectly round. You may have to sand the tubing with emery cloth to get the ferrule to slide on. Smear pipe joint compound on the ferrule and the male threads of the fitting.

2 TIGHTEN THE NUT.

Tighten the compression nut with a wrench, forcing the ferrule into the tubing to secure and seal the connection. If the joint leaks when the water is turned on, tighten the nut a quarter turn at a time until the leak stops. Be careful—too much pressure can crush the tubing or crack the nut.

YOU'LL NEED

TIME: About 15 minutes to make a simple connection.

SKILLS: No special skills needed.

TOOLS: Two adjustable wrenches.

Using compression fittings (continued)

Installing a compression union

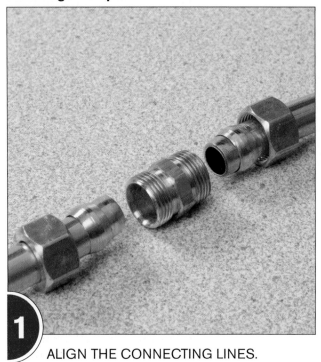

1 ALIGN THE CONNECTING LINES.

Bend the tubing sections into position (see page 146). Slip a nut and a ferrule onto each piece of tubing.

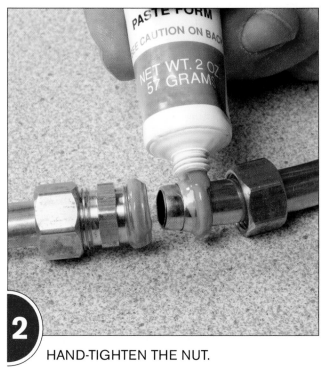

2 HAND-TIGHTEN THE NUT.

Apply pipe joint compound on the ferrules and on the male threads of the union. Slide the pieces together and hand-tighten the nut. Slide the compression ring and the nut against the valve threads. Hand-tighten the nut again.

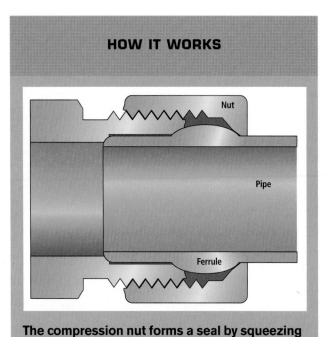

HOW IT WORKS

The compression nut forms a seal by squeezing the ferrule against the copper pipe. Because copper is a soft metal, the resulting seal is extremely tight. Still, use pipe joint compound to make sure the seal is watertight. Anchor or support the tubing within 2 feet of either side of the fitting.

3 TIGHTEN EACH SIDE.

Have one wrench grip the union and use another wrench to tighten each side. Once snug, tighten a half turn more. Turn on the water to check for leaks. If it leaks, gently tighten more.

USING FLARE FITTINGS

Flare fittings, like compression fittings, are useful in places where it's difficult to solder a joint. Don't hide flare fittings inside a wall. You can use flare fittings only with flexible copper tubing, not on rigid pipe. Unlike compression fittings, this type of fitting requires a flaring tool. The two-piece tool reshapes the end of the copper tubing, "flaring" it to fit into a special flare fitting. Sometimes the tubing splits while being flared so, if possible, make the flared connection first, then cut the tubing to length.

YOU'LL NEED

TIME: About 30 minutes to join two pieces together in a union.

SKILLS: Use of a flaring tool.

TOOLS: Flaring tool, adjustable wrenches.

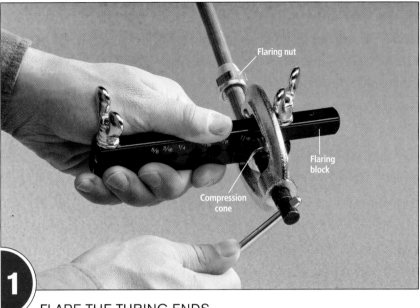

Flaring nut
Flaring block
Compression cone

1 FLARE THE TUBING ENDS.

The first thing to remember: Slip the flaring nut on before you flare the end of the tubing. Choose the hole in the flaring block that matches the outside diameter of the tubing. Clamp the tool onto the tubing. Align the compression cone on the tubing's end and tighten the screw. As you turn the handle, the cone flares the tubing's end. Inspect your work carefully after removing the tubing from the block. If the end has split, cut off the flared portion and repeat the process.

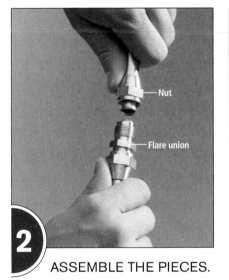

Nut
Flare union

2 ASSEMBLE THE PIECES.

Seat the flare union against one of the flared ends of the tubing, slide the nut down, and hand-tighten. Do the same on the other side. No pipe joint compound is necessary.

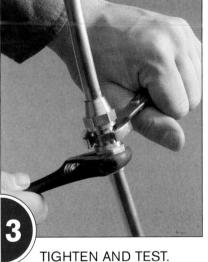

3 TIGHTEN AND TEST.

Place one wrench on the union and one on a nut. Don't overtighten a flared joint. Once snug, give each nut a half turn. Turn the water on and test. If the joint leaks, tighten it carefully until the leak stops. If the

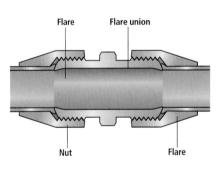

Flare   Flare union

Nut   Flare

leak persists, dismantle the joint and examine it to see if the tubing was cut squarely. Make sure that the nut was not cross-threaded on the fitting. Anchor or support the tubing within 2 feet of either side of the flare fitting.

REMOVING OLD THREADED PIPE

If you ever have to work with threaded pipe, you'll understand why this material is all but extinct in new installations. Cutting, threading, and assembling steel pipe requires muscle and specialized equipment. Sometimes when you're trying to take old pipe apart, you'll swear it is welded together.

If your home was built before World War II, its supply pipes are likely made of threaded steel. This doesn't mean you have to use the same pipe for improvements or repairs. Special fittings enable you to break into a line and add copper or plastic (see pages 134–135).

Black threaded pipe, which lacks the shiny grayness of galvanized pipe, is meant for gas only and is still commonly used. Don't use black pipe for water lines.

SWITCHING MATERIALS

If your plumbing supplies adequate water pressure and little rust is trapped in your aerators, there is no need to replace your threaded steel pipe with copper or plastic. But if water pressure is low, aerators fill up with rust, and leaks develop, it is time for a change. Replace long, horizontal lines first. Don't cut holes into walls and get involved in a major refit unless it is absolutely necessary.

YOU'LL NEED

TIME: About an hour to take apart four or five sections of pipe with fittings.

SKILLS: Use of a pipe wrench and sometimes brute strength.

TOOLS: Two pipe wrenches, hacksaw, maybe a propane torch.

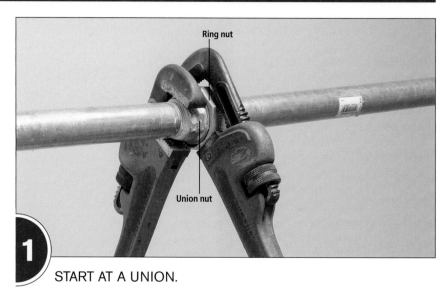

Ring nut

Union nut

1 START AT A UNION.

Shut off water and drain the pipes. Examine the way your pipes and fittings thread together, and you'll see that you can't begin unscrewing them just anywhere. Somewhere in every pipe run is a union that allows you to unlock and dismantle the piping. To crack open a union, determine which of the smaller union nuts the ring nut is threaded onto. With one wrench on each, turn the ring nut counterclockwise. Once it's unthreaded, you have the break you need and can start unscrewing pipes from fittings. When unscrewing pipe, use the second wrench to keep the fitting from turning.

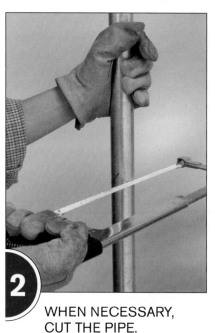

2 WHEN NECESSARY, CUT THE PIPE.

Without a union, you'll have to cut a pipe with a hacksaw or a reciprocating saw fitted with a metal-cutting blade. When you reassemble the run, you can install a union using prethreaded nipples on either side of the union.

3 IF THE PIPE WON'T BUDGE.

Stubborn joints may respond to penetrating oil, or you can try heating the fitting with a propane torch. Try a larger pipe wrench or slip a piece of 1¼-inch or 1½-inch pipe onto the handle of your wrench to increase its leverage.

INSTALLING THREADED PIPE

If you choose to work with threaded pipe, you'll face the difficulty of ending the run at the right place. Because the ends of the pipe are threaded, you can't simply cut a piece to fit, as you can with copper or plastic. Purchase long pieces that take up most of the runs and have on hand plenty of couplings and a selection of nipples or short lengths of pipe that are threaded on each end to give you options to end the run in the right spot.

BOOSTING PRESSURE

In an old house, galvanized pipes that are clogged with rust result in poor water pressure. If the problem is limited to one fixture, replace a few of the pipes that lead up to it. If the problem runs throughout the house, call in a professional.

There are companies that specialize in unclogging galvanized pipe. They use a process that causes rust and corrosion to fall away from the inside of the pipe. The process can take months to complete, will clog faucets, and may reveal leaks as the gunk is removed. In the end, however, water will flow through the pipes as if they were new.

YOU'LL NEED

TIME: In an hour you can assemble about four pipe lengths with fittings.

SKILLS: Pipe measuring, use of pipe wrench.

TOOLS: Tape measure, two pipe wrenches.

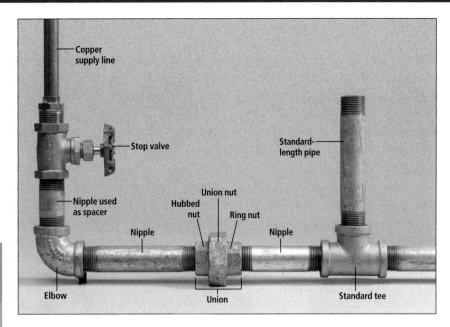

Copper supply line · Stop valve · Nipple used as spacer · Elbow · Nipple · Hubbed nut · Union nut · Ring nut · Union · Nipple · Standard-length pipe · Standard tee

ASSEMBLING THE PARTS.

This typical installation combines standard-length pipes with joints and nipples to end up exactly at the right location. (For background on measuring pipe accurately, see pages 136–137.) Many plumbing suppliers offer ready-cut galvanized pipe in standard sizes—12 inches, 48 inches, and so on—for less cost (and delay) than custom-cut pieces. Try to use standard-size pieces; if you make a mistake in measuring custom cuts, the store may refuse its return.

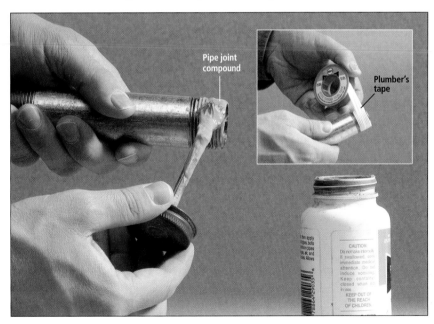

Pipe joint compound · Plumber's tape

JOINING THE PIECES.

Before you thread a pipe and fitting together, seal the pipe threads using pipe joint compound or plumber's tape. Assemble the pipes and fittings one at a time, tightening each as you go. If your assembly requires a union, work from each end toward the union. The union is installed last. Support runs of threaded pipe at least every 6 feet.

WORKING WITH RIGID PLASTIC PIPE

Plastic plumbing is popular with do-it-yourselfers because it is inexpensive and easy to work with. Plastic pipe cuts with an ordinary hacksaw and goes together without special tools or techniques. You simply clean the burrs from the cut, prime, and glue the parts together.

Still, installing plastic pipe requires attention to detail, planning ahead, and doing things in the right order. If you make a mistake, the parts can't be disassembled. You'll have to cut out the faulty section, throw it out, and start again.

You'll find various types of plastic, so check local codes to make sure you're using the right type for your purpose. In most localities, either ABS or PVC are accepted (sometimes even required) for drain lines. Many localities do not accept plastic pipe for supply lines; others specify CPVC (see pages 132–133). Do not mix ABS with PVC. Each expands at a different rate and requires a differently formulated cement. Plastic pipe is not as stiff as metal. Be sure to support horizontal runs every 4 to 5 feet.

YOU'LL NEED

TIME: With practice, you can cut and install about five fittings and five pieces of pipe in an hour.

SKILLS: Measuring, cutting, and assembling components in a logical manner.

TOOLS: Plastic pipe saw or hacksaw, miter box, tape measure, utility knife, pencil, emery cloth, plastic tubing cutter for supply lines.

1 MEASURE AND CUT.

When measuring pipe for cutting, take the socket depth of the fitting into account (see pages 136–137). Cut with any fine-tooth saw, using a miter box. Avoid diagonal cuts because they reduce the bonding area at the deepest part of the fitting's socket—the most critical part of the joint.

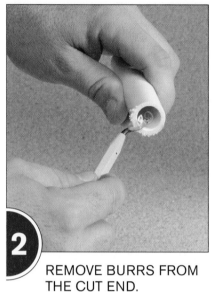

2 REMOVE BURRS FROM THE CUT END.

After you've made the cut, use a knife or file to remove any burrs from the inside and outside of the cut end. Burrs can scrape away cement when the pipe is pushed into the fitting, weakening the bond.

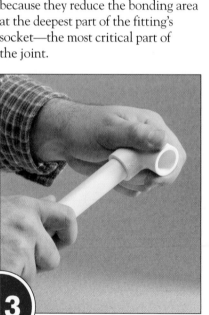

3 TEST THE FITTING.

Dry-fit the connection. You should be able to push it in at least one-third of the way. If the pipe bottoms out and feels loose, try another fitting. Unlike copper components, plastic pipes are designed with tapered walls on the inside of the socket so that the pipe makes contact well before it reaches the socket shoulder.

4 MARK FOR ALIGNMENT.

When gluing the pieces together, you will have less than a minute to correctly position the pipe and fitting before the glue sets. Draw an alignment mark across the pipe and fitting of each joint. When you fit the pieces together, the mark will indicate exactly how to position the pipe and fitting.

5 CLEAN AND PRIME.

Wipe the inside of the fitting and the outside of the pipe end with a clean cloth. If you are working with PVC or CPVC (but not ABS), coat the outside of the pipe end with a special primer. Many inspectors require purple-colored primer so they can easily see that joints have been primed.

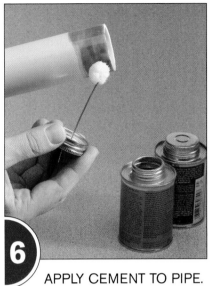

6 APPLY CEMENT TO PIPE.

Use the cement designed for the material you're working with. Immediately after you've primed, swab a smooth coating of cement onto the pipe end.

7 PRIME AND CEMENT FITTING.

Repeat the process on the inside of the fitting socket. Apply cement liberally but don't let it puddle inside the fitting. Reapply a coating of cement to the pipe end.

DRY-FIT THREE OR FOUR PIECES AHEAD

Whenever possible, cut and dry-fit three or four pieces before priming and gluing. That way, you can get things lined up ahead of time and avoid going back and forth between cans of primer and cement.

However, don't dry-fit more than four pieces and don't dry-fit an entire section that must come out to an exact length. Plastic is not like copper pipe, which will solder together exactly the way it was dry-fitted. Once the cement is applied, plastic pipes may slide farther in than they did during the dry run, throwing off measurements as much as ¼ inch per fitting.

8 TWIST AND HOLD.

Forcefully push the two together to ensure the pipe moves fully into the socket. Twist a quarter turn as you push to help spread the cement evenly. Complete the twist until your alignment marks come together. Hold the pipe and fitting together for about 20 seconds while they fuse into a single piece. Wipe away excess cement.

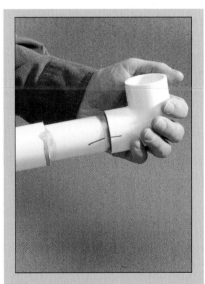

CUT OFF ANY INCORRECT JOINTS.

If you misalign a connection, saw it off squarely. Install a new fitting with a spacer and slip coupling, as shown. Cemented joints are strong enough to handle after 15 minutes, but don't run water in the line for about two hours.

WORKING WITH ABS PIPE

Many homes built in the 1960s and 1970s have ABS (acrylonitrile-butadiene-styrene) drainpipes. ABS is now banned for use in many locales, because it sometimes becomes brittle and/or shrinks, causing joints to leak. PVC is generally considered superior to ABS and is required by many local codes.

If your home has ABS pipe, you probably do not have to replace it. However, codes may require that you use PVC pipe for new installations. If so, be sure to use an approved ABS/PVC transition fitting when joining the new to the old. In many locales, it is difficult if not impossible to buy new ABS pipe.

If codes allow the use of ABS, cut and install it much as you would PVC pipe.

1 USE ABS CLEANER AND CEMENT.

Be sure to use products made for joining ABS—not PVC—pipe. "All purpose" cement and primer is not recommended. With ABS, you use a cleaner rather than a primer before applying the cement.

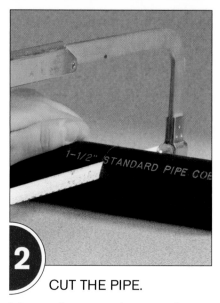

2 CUT THE PIPE.

Measure for cutting the pipe, taking into account the distance the pipe will travel inside the fittings. Cut ABS pipe using a hacksaw, a plastic pipe saw, or a power miter saw. Take care to make square cuts; an angled cut makes for a weak joint.

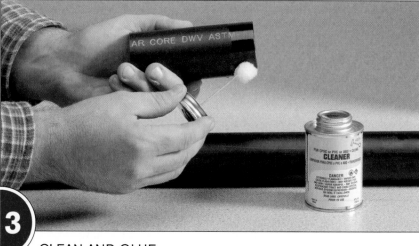

3 CLEAN AND GLUE.

Remove all burrs from the inside and outside of the pipe using a deburring tool, sandpaper, or a knife. Assemble a dry run of up to seven or eight pipes and fittings, to make sure they all fit. Draw alignment marks wherever a fitting needs to face in a certain direction.

Disassemble the dry run, placing the parts in order so you can easily reassemble. Wipe the pieces free of debris using a dry cloth. Apply ABS cleaner to the insides of the fittings and the outsides of the pipes.

Cement the joints one at a time. To make a connection, use the dauber to apply cement to the pipe end and to the inside of the fitting. Within a few seconds, insert the pipe into the fitting, twisting slightly as you push. Hold the fitting still for 10 seconds or so, then wipe away any excess cement. After all the pieces have been connected, wait a half hour or so before running water through them.

WORKING WITH CPVC/PEX

Chlorinated polyvinyl chloride (CPVC) pipe, tubing, and fittings can be used in both hot- and cold-water supply systems. CPVC is often the material of choice for outdoor installations. However, many local codes do not permit its use for interior installations; you may need to install copper instead. Some codes require special "proof testing" of CPVC assemblies; contact your local building inspector to find out if this is required.

WORKING WITH CPVC CHECKLIST

- Make sure all cements and pipe-thread tape are made for use with CPVC pipe.

- Keep all pipe and fittings in original packaging until needed.

- Use tools designed for use with plastic pipe and fittings.

- Cut all pipe ends square.

- Deburr and bevel the pipe ends of CPVC.

- Rotate the pipe at least ¼ turn when bottoming the pipe into the fitting socket.

- Avoid puddling cement in fittings and pipe.

- Follow the cement manufacturer's recommended cure times before pressure testing.

- Support the pipe with plastic pipe straps that fully encircle the pipe.

- When running pipe through wood studs, drill holes ¼ inch larger than the outside diameter of the tube.

- Use protective pipe isolators when running through metal studs.

1 USE THE RIGHT TOOLS AND MATERIALS.

Avoid "all-purpose" cement and primer and use products made specifically for joining CPVC pipe. Follow local codes. Most inspectors require highly visible purple primer, so they can quickly see that you have primed the joints. Choose cans that have daubers about half the diameter of the fittings. Larger daubers make a mess, and smaller daubers do not apply enough cement or primer. To quickly cut pipe, buy a pipe cutter made for use with your size pipe.

2 CUT, DEBURR, AND DRY-FIT.

Measure for pipe cuts, taking into account the distance the pipe will travel inside the fittings. Draw cut lines using a felt-tipped marker. Cut the pipe using a scissors-type cutter, a hacksaw, a pipe saw, or a power miter saw. Make the cuts square; an angled cut will weaken the joint. Use a pipe deburring tool, a knife, or a piece of sandpaper to remove the burrs. Assemble seven or eight pipes and fittings in a dry run. Once you are sure they all fit correctly, make alignment marks wherever a fitting needs to face a certain direction.

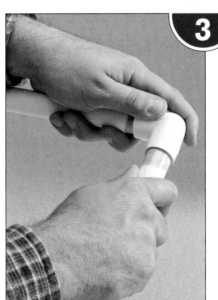

3 CEMENT A JOINT.

Disassemble the dry run and keep the parts in order. Wipe the pipes and fittings clean of debris using a dry cloth. Apply primer to the insides of the fittings and to the outsides of the pipe ends.

Cement the joints one at a time. Apply cement with a dauber, first to the inside of the fitting and then to the pipe end. Immediately insert the pipe into the fitting, twisting slightly as you push. Hold the fitting still for 10 seconds or so, then wipe away any excess cement. After all the pieces have been cemented, wait an hour or so before running water through them.

GLOSSARY

For words not listed here, or for more about those that are, refer to the index (pages 159–160).

ABS. Acrylonitrile-butadiene-styrene. A rigid black plastic pipe used predominately for drain-waste-vent (DWV) systems.

Access panel. A removable panel in a wall or ceiling that permits repair or replacement of concealed items such as faucet bodies.

Adapter. A fitting that makes it possible to go from male endings to female endings or vice-versa. Transition adapters allow for joining different kinds of pipe together in the same run. Trap adapters help connect drain lines to sink traps.

Aerator. A device screwed into the spout outlet of most sink faucets that mixes air with the water to achieve less water splash and smoother flow.

Air chamber. A short, enclosed tube on water lines that provides a cushion of air to control sudden surges in water pressure that sometimes result in noisy pipes.

Air gap. A device mounted on a kitchen sink which connects the drain line between a dishwasher and a disposal, allowing the dishwasher to discharge freely into the disposal while preventing water from siphoning back into the dishwasher. Check local codes.

Auger. A flexible metal cable fished into traps and drain lines to dislodge obstructions.

Ballcock. The assembly inside a toilet tank that, when activated, releases water into the bowl to start the flushing action. It also prepares the toilet for the subsequent flushes.

Ball valve. A valve using a ball to seal against the seat.

Basin wrench. A wrench with a long handle that has jaws mounted on a swivel. Used to reach tailpiece nuts that are difficult to reach with a normal wrench.

Blow bag. A device consisting of a rubber bladder with a hose fitting on one end and a nozzle on the other. When water is introduced with a hose, it expands to seat in the pipe and releases pulsating bursts of water using the force of the water to clear line blockages.

Check valve. A valve that prevents backflow occurring in a system that allows water to flow in only one direction.

Cleanout. A removable plug in a trap or a drainpipe that allows easier access to blockages inside.

Closet bend. The elbow-shaped fitting beneath toilets that carries waste to the main drain.

Codes. See Uniform Plumbing Code.

Compression fitting. A tubing or pipe connection where a nut and a sleeve or ferrule are placed over a copper or plastic tube and compressed tightly around the tube as the nut is tightened, forming a sealed joint without soldering.

Coupling. A fitting used to connect two lengths of pipe in a straight run.

Dielectric fitting. A fitting to join copper and steel pipe, insulating the pipes from an otherwise corrosive chemical reaction.

Drain-waste-vent (DWV) system. The network of pipes and fittings that carries liquid and solid wastes out of a building to a public sewer, a septic tank, or a cesspool. It also allows for the passage of sewer gases up through the roof and to the outside.

Drum trap. A canister trap used in sewer lines of older homes typically constructed of lead or cast iron.

Elbow. A fitting used to change the direction of a water supply line. Also known as an ell. Bends do the same thing with drain-waste-vent lines.

Fall. Used to express the slope at which drain lines are installed to ensure proper waste drainage. Minimum fall per foot is ¼ inch.

Fitting. Any connector (except a valve) that allows you to join pipes of similar or dissimilar size or material in a straight run or at an angle.

Fixture drain. The drainpipe and trap leading from a fixture to the main drain.

Flapper. The moving part of a flush valve that seals the water into the tank when closed or allows the water to exit when opened during the flush cycle.

Float ball. The ball connected to the ballcock inside the tank. The float ball rises or falls with the change in water level during the flush cycle.

Flux. A stiff jelly brushed or smeared on the surfaces of copper and brass pipes and fittings before soldering them to assist in the cleaning and bonding processes.

Grease trap. A trap that captures grease entering the drainpipe before it reaches the sewer. This type of trap requires periodic cleaning.

Hose bib. An outdoor faucet. Hose bibs can also be used as supply valves for a washing machine.

Increaser. A fitting used to enlarge a vent stack as it passes through the roof.

Inside diameter (ID). Almost all plumbing pipes are sized according to their inside diameter. See also Nominal size and Outside diameter.

Main drain. That portion of the drainage system between the fixture drains and the sewer drain. See also Fixture drain and Sewer drain.

Nipple. A 12-inch or shorter pipe that has threads on both ends that is used to join fittings. A close nipple has threads that run from both ends to the center.

No-hub pipe. A type of cast-iron pipe designed for use by do-it-yourselfers. Pipes and fittings are joined using stainless-steel clamps with rubber gaskets.

Nominal size. The designated dimension of a pipe or fitting. It varies slightly from the actual size. See also Inside diameter.

O-ring. A round rubber washer used to create a watertight seal, chiefly around valve stems.

Outside diameter (OD). Plumbing parts are rarely measured by their outside diameter, with flexible copper tubing being the primary exception. See also Inside diameter and Nominal size.

P trap. See trap.

Packing. An asbestos material (used mainly around faucet stems) that, when compressed, results in a watertight seal.

PB (polybutylene). A flexible plastic tubing used, where allowed by code, in water supply systems.

Pipe joint compound. A material applied to pipe threads to ensure a watertight seal. Also called pipe dope. See also Teflon tape.

Pipe-thread tape. A synthetic material wrapped around pipe threads to seal a joint. See also Pipe joint compound.

Plumber's putty. A doughlike material used as a sealant. Often a bead of it is around the underside of toilets and sinks.

Plunger. A suction-action tool used to dislodge obstructions from drain lines. Also called a force cup and a plumber's friend.

PSI (pounds per square inch). Water pressure is rated in PSIs.

PVC (polyvinyl chloride). A rigid white plastic pipe used in drain-waste-vent systems.

Reducer. A fitting with different-size openings at either end used to go from a larger to a smaller pipe.

Relief valve. A device designed to open if it senses excess temperature or pressure.

Riser. Any vertical plastic or metal pipe or assembly.

Rough-in. The early stages of a plumbing project during which supply and drain-waste-vent lines are run to their destinations. All work done after the rough-in is finish work.

Run. Any length of pipe or pipes and fittings going in a straight line.

Saddle tee. A fitting used to tap into a water line without having to break the line apart. Some local codes prohibit its use.

Saddle valve. A valve mounted on a pipe run by clamping a saddle to provide and control water supplying a low-demand appliance such as an icemaker.

Sanitary fitting. Any of several connectors used to join drain-waste-vent lines. Their design helps direct waste downward.

Sanitary sewer. Underground drainage network that carries liquid and solid waste to a treatment plant.

Septic tank. A reservoir that collects and separates liquid and solid waste, diverting the liquid waste onto a drainage field.

Sewer drain. That part of the drainage system that carries liquid and solid waste from a dwelling to a sanitary sewer, septic tank, or cesspool.

Shutoff valve. Normally used when referring to valve stops for sinks and toilets, but also refers to valves installed alongside the water meter and on branch lines.

Soil stack. A vertical drainpipe that carries waste toward the sewer drain. The main soil stack is the largest vertical drain line of a building into which liquid and solid waste from branch drains flow. See also Vent stack.

Soldering. A technique used to produce watertight joints between various types of metal pipes and fittings. Solder, when reduced to molten form by heat, fills the void between two metal surfaces and joins them together.

Solvent-welding. A technique used to produce watertight joints between plastic pipes and fittings. Chemical "cement" softens mating surfaces temporarily and enables them to meld into one.

Stop valve. A device installed in a water supply line, usually near a fixture, that lets you shut off the water supply to one fixture without interrupting service to the rest of the system.

Storm sewer. An underground drainage network designed to collect and carry away water from storm drains. See also Sanitary sewer.

Tailpiece. Part of a fixture drain that bridges the gap between the drain outlet and the trap.

Glossary (continued)

Tee. A T-shaped fitting used to tap into a length of pipe at a 90-degree angle for the purpose of beginning a branch line.

Thermocouple. A device used in a gas water heater to regulate and measure temperatures accurately. Thermocouples consist of two dissimilar metals joined so that a potential difference generated between the points of contact is a measure of the temperature difference between the points.

Trap. The part of a fixture drain that creates a water seal to prevent sewer gases from penetrating a home's interior. Codes require that all fixtures be trapped.

Uniform Plumbing Code. A nationally recognized set of guidelines prescribing safe plumbing practices. Local codes take precedence over this when the two differ.

Union. A fitting used to join pieces of threaded pipe.

Valve. A device to regulate the flow of water in a supply system or fixture.

Valve seat. The non-moving part of a valve. The flow of water is stopped when the stem or moveable part of the valve comes in contact with the valve seat.

Vent. The vertical or sloping horizontal portion of a drain line that permits sewer gases to exit the house. Every fixture in a house must be vented.

Vent stack. The upper portion of a vertical drain line through which gases pass directly to the outside. The main vent stack is the portion of the main vertical drain line above the highest fixture connected to it.

Water hammer. A loud noise caused by a sudden stop in the flow of water, which causes pipes to repeatedly hit up against a nearby framing member.

Water hammer arrestor. A device installed at an appliance or fixture to absorb the hydraulic shock created by a sudden shutoff of water, such as occurs when operating a clothes washer.

Water supply system. The network of pipes and fittings that transports water under pressure to fixtures and other water-using equipment and appliances.

Wet wall. A strategically placed cavity (usually a 2×6 wall) in which the main drain/vent stack and a cluster of supply and drain-waste-vent lines are housed.

Wye. A Y-shaped drainage fitting that serves as the starting point for a branch drain supplying one or more fixtures.

METRIC CONVERSIONS

U.S. Units to Metric Equivalents

To convert from	Multiply by	To Get
Inches	25.4	Millimeters
Inches	2.54	Centimeters
Feet	30.48	Centimeters
Feet	.03048	Meters
Yards	.9144	Meters
Miles	1.6093	Kilometers
Square inches	6.4516	Square centimeters
Square feet	0.0929	Square meters
Square yards	0.8361	Square meters
Acres	0.4047	Hectares
Square miles	2.5899	Square kilometers
Cubic inches	16.387	Cubic centimeters
Cubic feet	0.0283	Cubic meters
Cubic feet	28.316	Liters
Cubic yards	0.7646	Cubic meters
Cubic yards	764.55	Liters

To convert from degrees Fahrenheit (F) to degrees Celsius (C), first subtract 32, then multiply by $\frac{5}{9}$.

Metric Units to U.S. Equivalents

To convert from	Multiply by	To Get
Millimeters	0.0394	Inches
Centimeters	0.3937	Inches
Centimeters	0.0328	Feet
Meters	3.2808	Feet
Meters	1.0936	Yards
Kilometers	0.6214	Miles
Square centimeters	0.1550	Square inches
Square meters	10.764	Square feet
Square meters	1.1960	Square yards
Hectares	2.4711	Acres
Square kilometers	0.3861	Square miles
Cubic centimeters	0.0610	Cubic inches
Cubic meters	35.315	Cubic feet
Liters	0.0353	Cubic feet
Cubic meters	1.038U	Cubic yards
Liters	0.0013	Cubic yards

To convert from degrees Celsius to degrees Fahrenheit, multiply by $\frac{9}{5}$, then add 32.

INDEX

Index *(continued)*